GW00720556

INSIGHTS

TO DEVELOP YOUR PROFESSIONAL AND PERSONAL LIFE

LID

LONDON	NEW YORK	SHANGHAI
MADRID	BARCELONA	BOGOTA
MEXICO CITY	MONTERREY	BUENOS AIRES

Published by
LID Publishing Limited,
The Record Hall, Studio 204,
16-16a Baldwins Gardens,
London EC1N 7RJ, UK

524 Broadway, 11th Floor, Suite 08-120
New York, NY 10012, US

info@lidpublishing.com
www.lidpublishing.com

A member of:

www.businesspublishersroundtable.com

© LID Publishing Limited, 2018

Printed in Great Britain by TJ International
ISBN: 978-1-911498-70-4

Editorial Director: Sara Taheri
Cover and page design: Caroline Li and Matthew Renaudin

CONTENTS

INTRODUCTION

In the 25 years since the foundation of LID, we have helped over 3,000 authors convey their ideas and knowledge to millions of readers like you. This book is a testament to and recognition of all these authors, though we could only include 250 in these pages.

As Steve Jobs said, good ideas are created by connecting the dots. That is why we invite you to read these insights, to cross your own experience with that of our authors.

There is no particular order in which these insights have been presented, but each has been carefully selected to lead you on an inspirational journey. We believe that if you read one text each day you will come across real breakthrough and your effort will be paid back generously.

To experience and to learn is human nature and our desire is to facilitate this for you.

Thank you so much for following and supporting us. We hope that our common journey will be long and fruitful.

Marcelino Elosua,
Founder & CEO

TOTAL COMMITMENT

Change has a way of bringing out the best, the worst and the 'so-so' in people. The 'iffy' behaviour – this 'so-so' stuff – occurs when people make a habit out of shaving standards and dropping them, in their efforts to cope.

Pressed to keep up with change – to do more with less – some people play fast and loose. They shrug off the idea of excellence in an effort to pick up a little speed.

Scrambling to cover the necessary ground, they make sacrifices in the quality of their performance. If everyone was playing to their Spikes, the collaboration and interdependency would catch this careless behaviour instantly.

The slippage begins when employees cut themselves some slack. They excuse themselves for giving less than their best and thus create a culture of mediocrity.

Considering the circumstances – the pressure, the stress, all the new demands – they rationalize that it's okay to go the quick-and-dirty route, to settle for lower commitment to their work – or to relax on issues relating to ethics and integrity.

What's your personal vision or mantra that keeps you full of hope and moving forward every day?

– *SPIKE,* René Carayol

DARKNESS ILLUMINATES

It follows that if knowing is good, then its opposite is bad. It's a simple matter of logic for most people. But when we use the term Not Knowing we aren't talking about the common view of those two words, but rather the ancient 'apophatic tradition' used to describe what something was 'not' rather than what it was. In this spirit, we are distinguishing Not Knowing from the position of the absence of knowledge (otherwise known as ignorance), and from partial knowledge that can be discovered.

A common contemporary metaphor associates knowledge with light and Not Knowing with darkness. This is illustrated by the phrase, "I'm in the dark." Paradoxically, Not Knowing often leads to learning and new knowledge. Just as in nature and biology, Not Knowing can lead to growth that is unseen, like the embryo in the womb or the seed deep in the earth.

We are tempted to think that nothing is happening when it is not easily visible, yet transformation is unfolding, in the dark. We tend to place more value on the seen, things in the metaphorical light, but nature presents a perfect balance of day and night. Admitting that we don't know allows us to learn. The darkness of Not Knowing creates the freedom and space for new sources of illumination.

– Not Knowing,
Steven D'Souza & Diana Renner

When was the last time you said, "I don't know?" Where can you adopt a 'beginner's mind'?

LONELINESS

Managers often complain that they experience loneliness. We should make a distinction between reasonable loneliness, such as the type experienced by a captain who steers a ship, and a more pernicious form of loneliness, such as the type resulting from someone having taken a poor course of action which creates a distance from others. In most cases, the fundamental obstacle comes from a lack of knowledge on how to train collaborators. Perhaps they are on their knees – looking to pay tribute – while failing to grasp the good intention and intelligence of those on whom they should have relied. Good collaborators should not only perform dictated instructions.

More often than not, loneliness is a consequence of another lacking factor, of activities of certain positions systematically ignored for months, if not years. According to Shakespeare's description, Richard II was already on the threshold of death by the time he discovered a truth that would help him rule with more humanity, the kind that would make for more tolerable dynamics between ruler and ruled:

Be aware of the difference between solitude that favours decision-making and isolation that distances.

"I live with bread like you," the monarch cried out; "feel want, taste grief, need friends..."

– *La Soledad del Directivo*,
Javier Fernández Aguado
& José Aguilar

THEATRE OF ACTION

The focal point of several kinds of operation is described as a 'theatre': the place where the crucial action happens – the stage, the operating theatre, the theatre of war, for example. In all of these theatres, there is a clear recognition that the most important people are those closest to the action: the actors; technicians; stage-hands; surgeons; anaesthetists; nurses; soldiers; tank drivers. Seniority, in the traditional sense, tends to increase as we move away from the actual theatre. The job of senior executives at the head of theatrical companies and hospitals and armies is to frame the overall strategy and to keep the organization running smoothly, but these people will – or should – be acutely aware that it is what happens in the theatre that is of defining importance.

This is a useful frame of mind. Where – in both our personal and our professional lives – is our theatre of action? Where is the beating heart of what we do? The key to finding the right answer is to focus on the essential outcome, the bit that really matters. A well-disciplined and perfectly supplied army that cannot win battles in the theatre of war is not a good army. A brilliantly run theatre group that cannot put on an audience-pleasing show is not a successful theatre group.

– Perform to Win,
Dr Mark Powell & Jonathan Gifford

Once it is obvious where our real theatre of action is located, it becomes clear who the key people are.

NAMING AND IDENTITIES

Brand naming and brand design are two different but equally important marketing disciplines. They are at the heart of many classical definitions of a brand. For example, Philip Kotler in *Managing Markets* defines a brand as: "A name, term, symbol or design, or a combination of them, which is intended to signify the goods or services of one seller or group of sellers, and to differentiate them from those of competitors."

Naming has come a long way. We take the strategies and stories behind brand names for granted. In fact, they are often a delightful mix of the rational and the strange. They provide inspiration and ideas for anyone face with the challenge of naming their own brand.

Beauty is in the eye of the beholder, or so they say, but the best designs do more than just identify a brand – they signify meaning.

– How Coca-Cola Took Over the World,
Giles Lury

THE COMMON GOAL

What happens when a waiter warns against a certain dish –"the chicken is a little dry tonight" – and then goes on to suggest lower-priced options? Suddenly the restaurant patrons feel their incentives are aligned with the waiter's motives – and that the waiter has their best interests at heart.

A demonstration that we are willing to sacrifice some income for the benefit of the other party can be an incredibly powerful act; it redefines the relationship from that of buyer and seller to buyer and adviser. The patrons now trust the waiter's intentions implicitly.

Somewhat ironically, this gives the waiter an opportunity to upsell wine and dessert, and probably earn higher tips.

This type of increased trust is easily achieved in a person-to-person setup. But what about corporations?

The public has seen enough examples of bad behaviour to taint its view of corporations as a whole. Rather than entering the relationship based on real trust, as we would with another human being, we enter the relationship expecting to be disappointed, let down, or, even worse, exploited.

> **Companies demonstrate aligned incentives by recommending things that are clearly not in their best interest.**

– Dan Ariely & Logan Ury
for *Dialogue*

CONTROLLING DIRECTION

Executive function is involved in planning, organizing, time management, creativity and thinking out of the box. It enables you to complete tasks that require forward thinking and has a controlling function over other cognitive domains to develop strategies and inhibit unwanted impulses.

Additionally, executive function plays an overarching role in meta-cognition. This is activities such as self-monitoring, self-control and self-evaluation. Executive function can inhibit impulses that, on consideration, prove not to be in your best interests, nor in the best interests of your company, community, or family. This can sometimes cause its own tensions depending where your greatest loyalty lies.

Executive function enables you to consider the implication of your actions before you enact them. It enables you to manage your emotions and monitor your thoughts in order to work more efficiently and effectively.

If executive function is your core cognitive strength, then you are the 'pilot'. You are in control of the direction of your company or organization.

Leadership and management skills are based on behaviour and, in turn, on cognitive fitness.

– *Executive Function,*
Keiron Sparrowhawk

OPPORTUNITY

The future belongs to those companies it is worth working for and not to those that are merely out to make money. It also belongs to those leaders who are focused on the common good and not those who are in it for their self-interest alone. The mindset with which these managers work – their virtues, their way of relating, the meaning they give to what they do, the principles inspiring them, the scope of their outlook by which they construe reality – will play a leading role in the creation of companies with a successful future.

We are all encouraged to pursue the common good and travel the adventure known as life, discovering our potential talent for leadership within it. After all, this is nothing more than intelligence in action. Over the course of time, we must learn to use our assets for something beyond individual interests, regardless of how legitimate they may be.

You can only conquer the future with structures that combine clarity with the goal of transparency, teamwork and decentralization.

– Liderar Para el Bien Común,
Luis Huete

SELF-TURMOIL

No enterprise can withstand a long-term ordeal. If you want to, you must put yourself through a constant state of turmoil. Don't blame the market. It's better to take a good hard look at yourself. Crisis is coming. Actually, in times of crisis, it is not company staff who should be reassessed. Rather, there are two other things we should reassess. The first is the CEO and the second is the company itself – whether its original culture can withstand the times. How should we assess the CEO? What is a CEO?

Everyone knows that a CEO is principally in charge of two tasks. When times are good, the CEO must make decisions about which things are not worthwhile and must be got rid of. They are disasters waiting to happen if they are not eliminated. In times of difficulty, the CEO must find where opportunities lie. When your staff have full confidence in the CEO, he must be careful, and when they are showing signs of grievances, he must seek out opportunities. This is the CEO, this is a leader, they have ultimate responsibility. Only a leader can carry out this kind of duty. A professional manager does not think much about problems like these. The mark of a true CEO is foresight, open-mindedness and strength.

Foresight is the perspective, depth and breadth with which you look at a problem.

– *Jack Ma & Alibaba,*
Yan Qicheng

HALT!

Halt – hungry, angry, lonely, tired.

Be honest with yourself. If your state of mind falls into any of the four above categories, leave the decision for another day. You are simply not up to making a call. One of the paradoxes of modern business life is that company cultures and regulatory pressures can make it less likely that executives are in the sort of mental shape needed to make decisions. "The constant grind of the short term and the operational, and focusing on regulatory issues, can cause people to think constantly about the day-to-day," says Camelia Ram, a consultant with Decision Strategies International who specializes in improving decision-making processes in financial services organizations. "Some people are asked to tick all these boxes – and therefore do not have the time or energy to step back. It's important that companies recognize that intense focus on the day-to-day is likely to significantly reduce their power to think strategically."

There's a common British English idiom that is instructive here: "Sleep on it."

Defer your decision making until you feel fresher.

Thinking clearly is harder than you might assume.

– Ben Walker for *Dialogue*

CERVANTES AND FREEDOM

Cervantes knew prison and, in his novel *Don Quixote*, he sings about freedom: "Nothing on earth, in my opinion, equals happiness as the attainment of a freedom once lost." Freeing the slaves from the galley, the nobleman proclaims: "It's hard for me to enslave those whom God and nature have born free."

He shares a common distrust of liberals, one that took shape in the 18th century with Adam Smith, the Scottish Enlightenment and the theory of unintended consequences. It happened with Andrés, the waiter who was tied to the oak tree and whipped, who reappears later to denounce the harmful consequences of quixotic interventionism. Individual responsibility, in itself, becomes a principle for the hero: "Know yourself, Sancho, you are not a man more important than another if you do not do more than another." *Quixote* is also a Smithian work, *avant la lettre*, in its depiction of an archaic economy generating a surplus which, when not swapped, gives rise to both fabulous hospitality, such as Camacho's, and to public entertainment.

We can learn economy and value freedom by reading the great literary classics.

– *Diez Ensayos Liberales II*,
Carlos Rodríguez Braun

WE ARE IMMORTAL

Every day we are transmitting packages of our data through internet channels. But it's not a simple transmission. It is received, transmitted, processed, reprocessed, filtered, connected, reconnected, aggregated, matched and stored (actions that are just the tip of the 'connectivity iceberg') at an astonishing rate. And the motives for our data donation change minute by minute. We give it away for free, for commercial use and for reward, as we are now aware that our data connects and reconnects with other data that is useful to both sender and receiver.

What we watch, where we live, where we go, what we buy, who we talk to and what we search all become forms of stored and retransmitted data.

Broadly speaking, this stored data is either 'structured' (such as point-of-sale data when your credit card or loyalty card is swiped, census data, zip codes, or GPS data) or 'unstructured' (like social chat, e-mails, videos and photos). Human-to-human contact, connection and correspondence are clearly more about data-to-data flow as they are a flesh-to-flesh handshake, or eye-to-eye contact.

We are data because we can convert our thoughts, actions and desires into a digital format.

– *Upgraded,*
Andy Law

UPDATE FEEDBACK CULTURE

The truth is that we change and update our beliefs about how this world works all the time. A danger of that is that we are also more likely to be influenced by the 'bright, shiny objects' or 'trends du jour' – psychologists call these 'salience' and 'recency' effects. HR must guard organizations and their leaders from such cognitive biases and work hard on building beliefs based on proven scientific evidence.

Traditional cognitive psychology tells us that 'belief updating' has a sequential nature. We receive information piece by piece, then we form impressions that grow and change over time and, if we sufficiently repeat the same process with similar information, it becomes a belief. Herminia Ibarra brings to the fore the idea of 'outsight': behaving like a leader first will lead you to start thinking like one. This brings us to an updated formula that explains how people come to hold certain beliefs: "I know" – "I say" – "I do" – "I believe".

Following this formula, HR must equip organizations with the facts about performance feedback, design easily repeatable smart talent processes, support leaders to craft quality feedback and finally require leaders to share it, consistently.

Good feedback is a crucial element in individual and organizational performance.

– Sergey Gorbatov &
Angela Lane for *Dialogue*

LEARN FROM NATURE

We tend to learn from nature because we are of it. In particular, we are drawn to the realms of animals, birds, fish and insects, studying their behaviours and actions, borrowing from them in our folk tales, mythologies, poetry, fiction, even our business literature. In his book, *The Meaning of Human Existence*, E. O. Wilson points to humanity's anthropocentricity, our fascination with both ourselves and others like us. We project our humanity on to other things, other creatures, in order to sense-make and explain. This is common knowledge for students of myth and human storytelling through the ages. It informs our understanding of narratives about Little Red Riding Hood's lupine encounters, Gregor Samsa's metamorphosis, Aslan's wanderings through Narnia and the adventures of Rat, Mole, Badger and Toad.

The attraction of metaphors drawn from the natural world applies as much to those who perceive humankind to be at the centre of the universe as it does to advocates of Gaia theory, who recognise the Earth as a self-regulating system and maintain that humanity has no more value or meaning than any other life form. The metaphors expose the porousness of boundaries, serving as bridges between apparently contrarian views.

– *The Neo-Generalist*,
Kenneth Mikkelsen
& Richard Martin

It is an apt metaphor for the manner in which we can shift repeatedly from generalism to specialism.

DESIRABLE OUTCOMES

Signifying people, 'great leadership' touches on the most essential question in organizational change: who is going to enforce the change? The corresponding principle is 'starting from me', a foundation for grassroots change.

Signifying knowledge, 'sincerity' touches upon two fundamental questions in organizational change: *what* is the change for and *who* is it for? The corresponding principle is recognizing one's fallibility, a prerequisite of knowledge.

Signifying actions, 'practice' touches upon two fundamental factors in organizational change: when and where to start it, and how. The corresponding principle is people-centred. Change is essentially directed at people – more specifically, human psychologies and behaviours that should be changed.

Signifying perseverance, 'prudent beginnings and endings' touches upon two other matters in organizational change: persistence and improvement. The corresponding principle is 'continuous learning', the engine that sustains organizational change.

Desirable outcomes of corporate change are a result of four factors and cannot be achieved without the presence of all of them.

– *The Haier Model*,
Yangfeng Cao

LEARNING

Our day-to-day experiences provide us with an inexhaustible source of learning. What's important is not to miss such opportunities and, further, to reflect on them.

The greater the failure, the greater the possibility of learning.

Let's agree that for ten minutes a day, at the very least, we are a bunch of idiots. We must always have a Jiminy Cricket at the ready reminding us of this: what we are in those ten minutes.

We must find in ourselves our true worth – i.e. "I know I'm much more handsome when I don't feel ugly."

People's worth isn't assessed by what they own but by how they've achieved it. If we don't have dreams, if we're unable to get passionate about what we'd like to achieve, reaching it is going to be more than challenging.

Maturity is accepting the fact that you won't be able to appeal to everyone.

– *Cuentos que mi Jefe Nunca me Contó,*
Juan Mateo

COMPETE OR CREATE

We can choose to compete – from the Latin *com petare*, strive together – a social exercise wherein we compare ourselves to others and try to fit in and excel. Winning is awesome. In sports you get a medal when you win. In business, winning is associated with bumper profits and champagne. The feedback loop for competition is rather pleasant – we get to race, excel and win.

The other path is to create, a much less comfortable endeavour. The reason is that we tend to be sceptical when somebody creates something new – be it a work of art, a new technology, a new medical practice – and say things like "it won't work" or "you must be mad". If the initial scepticism is overcome and the idea gains some popularity, it will polarize people. Some will love you – for being brave and doing new things – whereas others will hate you, oppose you, ridicule you, maybe even try to kill you. Creation is a lonely path, full of obstacles and often without a clear goal. We have two paths to choose from – compete or create – but one of them seduces far more people with its promises of champagne, popularity and strive-togetherness.

We can choose between two paths in how we work, live and thrive.

– *Minifesto,*
Magnus Lindkvist

FACTS-BASED DECISIONS

Every cult needs its followers. The employees need to not only believe in the vision and values, but must have a clear understanding of what behaviour is required of them in order to thrive in the organization and why these beliefs and behaviours will make the organization serve its customers better. The organisation needs to ensure that these employee behaviours are embedded into every element of the employee lifecycle, especially recruitment, on-boarding and performance reviews. There needs to be cult-like 'organ rejection' of employees that do not 'fit' and exhibit the right behaviours. The organization, as a result, is full of people with the same value set, so it is engaging and empowering to work in.

Doing the right thing for customers and ensuring that they are happy needs to be an obsession. Therefore, organisations need to be clear on the needs of their customers, ensuring that they understand the 'Fundamental Truths' of what their customers need. They must then ensure they have a balanced suite of metrics that ensure that they understand how they are doing for customers, and more importantly helps them understand what they need to do to improve...it's the virtuous cycle of customer improvement.

The most significant outcomes from great Service Leadership are trust and respect.

– The Cult of Service Excellence,
Oke Eleazu

THE BOARD OF DIRECTORS

Companies rely on rigid models: the balance sheet, the profit and loss statement, the flow of funds and so on. For less quantitative assessments such as strategy formulation, the management of people, operations, commerce and finance, the relationship among various actors of capital markets, and innovation and control of the whole, they rely on more flexible systems. For this reason, accurate information must be collected and turned into reports. This allows management to follow up and guarantee through internal audits that their actions reflect the reality of their given situation, and that their company is complying with those regulations that could impact its activities.

The board of directors must ensure that all these processes flow correctly and efficiently. Furthermore, this concern has become a key topic in the leadership of companies, in the stimulus of a solid strategy, in achieving an optimal creation of values, in developing an appropriate culture with standards and social responsibility, and in disseminating ethical and legal standards in all the places where the company operates. This preoccupation fosters change and even the formulation of new regulations.

What aspects do you believe are essential for a board of directors looking to a 2020 horizon?

– *El Consejo 2020,*
Pedro Nueno

FIND YOUR WHY

There's nothing wrong with chasing perfection, universal adulation or fame and fortune. For many, these chases can be some of the most compelling motivators to launch. However, if they are the only goals for the launch, they aren't going to be enough to sustain you through the ups and downs of the journey.

First, these outcomes are unpredictable and not fully within your control. And then, even if you were able to reach them, you may discover a brief jolt of elation but they won't be entirely fulfilling. Such is the way of vanity chases.

The secret for the most successful launchers I know is that they have found the 'why', the compelling factor of their launch journeys. And that why is something meaningful. The end goal ceases to be an end-all, but rather a means to a greater end. They may not have always known what that why was at the beginning of the launch process, but they discover it somewhere along the journey.

– *The Launch Book*, Sanyin Siang

'Why' not only gives you and others clarity for the launch, but also gives you goals worth pursuing.

TOGETHER SOCIETY

We, the older generation, as we have more time to reflect, should say loud and clear: "Future generations, we have to leave you a world that's different from its current appearance. We have to make sure that society is more interconnected." I try to make suggestions at conferences or political roundtables: "We abolished mandatory military service, but why don't we establish a mandatory social year for men and women between the ages of 16 and 21?" I always listen to the same, massive counter-arguments: "Oh my god, we will never be able to get this through. First, we take away a year of a young person's training, and second we can't expect social engagement from everyone. Also, special training is required for social services." If we want to bring society more together, we must know that the glue holding things together is not watching a football game in Munich's Allianz Arena, or the common experience of a traffic jam.

Is it possible to simply take away the material blessings of the last 70 years?

– Pushing the Boundaries,
Herbert Henzler

NEED FOR SPEED

In the 1990s, the chief executive of the software company Oracle, Larry Ellison, had an infamous dictum – the 24-hour rule – that made it clear that if you didn't respond to an email within 24 hours you'd be out of a job. In 2018, that seems quaint. Twenty-four hours? If you don't reply to an email within 24 minutes nowadays you're considered a loser – a B-player in an organization that only hires A-players.

Information travels around the world in a fraction of a second. Ideas spread from San Francisco to Singapore as fast as they do to Sacramento. People fly from Sydney to Beijing for a lunch meeting and then turn around and go straight back home. Every aspect of the modern world is speeding up – this exponential curve we are in, which shows no sign of faltering – is unprecedented across the long arc of man's existence. As Canadian Prime Minister Justin Trudeau put it at the World Economic Forum in January 2018, "The pace of change has never been this fast, yet it will never be this slow again."

Calculate the future of work with one algorithm: Density x Complexity x Speed

– Ben Pring for *Dialogue*

A POSSIBILIST ATTITUDE

Pessimists look smart because they see problems everywhere.

They even like it when things go wrong because it proves they were right to be pessimistic.

Optimists look stupid because they think everything can be done.

It is easy for cynics to laugh at their apparently blind enthusiasm.

Possibilists can strike a balance between the two.

What's the best possible thing we could do here?

In geography circles, possibilism proposes that culture and human agency determine human behaviour rather than the environment (as environmental determinists would have us believe).

Possibilists believe they can find an intelligent way through – staying positive while remaining pragmatic.

Most things work out fine, so let's start by assuming that they will.

– *The Excellence Book,*
Kevin Duncan

FANCIFUL IMAGINATION

Imagination allows us to travel to the past and the future. Experimental psychologists point out that people maintain alternative realities, doing so in very different ways. One's emotional character, level of motivation, specific personality traits and cognitive differences in spatial and linguistic skills, as well as observational and operative memory capacity (which derive from the natural predisposition and the experiences of each person) result in radically different ways of perceiving reality, sometimes contrary to the majority.

For example, social experiments have found that a minority of participants always have the systematic ability to imagine remote possibilities and unlikely future scenarios, to generate combinations of intuitive and unexpected concepts, to take advantage of the knowledge generated by diving into others' perspectives. In this way, they can accurately predict the opinions of others in a possible future situation. This ability allows them to remain optimistic in the face of difficulties, hard data and otherwise disturbing information.

– La Siete Llaves de la Imaginación,
Piero Morosini

Using your imagination and thinking of potential solutions, rather than just focusing on the problems, can help you remain optimistic.

NEGOTIATION STYLES

In order to fully understand what makes your counterpart tick, you need to try and identify their particular negotiating style. You can only achieve this by putting your emotions to one side and thinking objectively. If you do not know their negotiating style, be creative about how you can discern it. You will get valuable clues from the culture of the organization, other contacts you have in common and people whom you know are in similar situations.

If you have negotiated with them before, look back on previous scenarios to gain greater insight. Similarly, think about how they behaved and notice any cues that will give you an indication of how they will behave when you negotiate. For example, when I attended sales meetings with retailers, I trained myself to notice the signs when they wanted investment from us by spotting a change in their approach and pitch. It is vital that you use this knowledge as part of your preparation for the negotiation stage as it will help you feel you are on a level playing field.

Understanding what truly motivates someone – both commercially and personally – can help you influence them.

– *The Negotiation Book,*
Nicole Soames

IDEA
BROKER

Idea brokerage is a powerful tool for fostering everyday innovation. This is very simply the idea that many of the things we think of as being 'creative' are in fact the blending or combination of pre-existing ideas.

Uber, the taxi app, has gained a lot of credit for being a revolutionary concept – and it is. But if you look at its component parts, it's the combination of several well-known functionalities used to tackle a well-known problem. The same is true of virtually any high-profile 'breakthrough' idea.

Be an idea broker:

1. Spot bright spots. Rather than focusing only on the problems, become a collector of interesting ideas and solutions;

2. Act as an intellectual 'middle-person'. Having spotted good ideas, move them around. Don't hoard ideas for yourself, but share ideas from different departments, companies and industries;

3. Embrace anxiety. Impulsively look for the 'injection of novelty' your situation needs.

Idea-making can be once a day rather than once in a lifetime.

– Tom Hughes for *Dialogue*

BUSINESS SURVIVAL

It is not impossible for an organization that once flew high and now experiences difficulties to rise again and get a second wind. There are no magic bullets to overcoming all hurdles, except the 'deathbed rescue' model which opens a genuine path for progress in business. You only have to follow three simple steps to take the reins and change course:

First step. Ask yourself: "What is the history behind the need to transform?" History arises when everyone feels the urgency of the current situation, though not without visualizing a bright future.

Second step. Make sure that everyone is on the same page: the leader, resolute and involved, willing to face challenges and capable of doing so; the management team that surrounds him, fully aligned; and a template so that each and every worker pushes and pulls in the right direction.

Third step. Implement a coherent and steadfast execution. The development and performance of a flexible strategy will ensure that results are not achieved through magic but through tenacity, courage and flexibility.

Sustainable change requires everyone to be on the same page and committed to the agreed strategy.

– *Salvados in Extremis,*
Bernardo Quinn

DEVELOPING SELF-CONFIDENCE

Self-confidence is a necessity for significant success for us and for our clients. Unfortunately, the fact that it is a necessity doesn't in itself tell us how to acquire this important trait.

Sure, most who have already achieved great success usually have self-confidence. Unfortunately, those who are not in this category – and that's most of us as we progress in our careers – sometimes feel self-confident, but many times we do not. We are concerned with possibly losing our jobs in tough times and we may sometimes choose the safest path when the way to enormous success involves more risk than we're willing to tolerate. We know what Drucker recommended to us and we may agree with his recommendations. We know that if we were achieving the success of that small percentage of our colleagues that are shooting ahead at light speed, we would have the self-confidence that Drucker wrote about. However, to reach that kind of success, we first need to acquire self-confidence. We can't achieve great things without self-confidence, but we can't have the self-confidence without achieving them first. Or so it would seem.

You must acquire self-confidence yourself before you can instil it in others.

– Consulting Drucker,
Dr William A. Cohen

GOODBYE, HOUDINI

Do you come out of meetings wondering what the meeting was about? Are you invited to meetings because the team needs your approval, or have you been invited for your input? Have you ever entered a crowded company elevator and asked yourself "what do these people do?" When you are in a meeting, have you ever thought "haven't we already covered this?"

If you are still reading this, you are probably infected with corporate escapism.

Take a step back from the process of decision-making and look at the context in which decisions are made. A pattern emerges. In many cases, our avoidance of the decision is due to the fact it is a reactive decision. A condition or event has occurred; a decision to course-correct is needed; this decision is counter to the status quo – or more precisely – to the plan we are currently executing. That reactive leadership appears disassociated from the strategy or plan, making the senior executive seem not fully in control of the organization.

The first step to curing this condition is to recognize that you have the disease.

The cure for management escapism is called 'leadership'.

– Joe DiVanna for *Dialogue*

WORKPLACE WELLBEING

The goal of improving the wellbeing of building occupants is an incredibly powerful change tool. We mentioned, when discussing why we needed to create a fantastic workplace, that the Elemental Workplace is itself a framework for wellbeing, in that a number of the Elements create conditions beneficial to wellbeing in the workplace, while a number of others create the possibility of our making better choices and decisions. We can now segregate the Elements accordingly and expand on that thinking.

If our inclusive workplace is flooded with natural daylight, if there is sufficient space with comfortable and ergonomic settings, if it is inspiring and stimulates the senses and our technology connects us seamlessly to the networks and highways we need, if we can use well-stocked and pleasant washrooms and store our stuff securely, then we are going to feel considerably more positive about our place of work, our colleagues and ourselves. Our physical condition and frame of mind are being looked after. It is playing to our wellbeing. We do not need to do anything, it is just happening for our benefit.

We can take a personal responsibility for our wellbeing, and have that enabled and respected by the organization.

– *The Elemental Workplace,*
Neil Usher

IMPORTANCE OF STRENGTHS

Have you ever felt like you were trying to be something you're not? Or that you were doing a job where you were expected to be something you're not?

Chances are that you were feeling this way because you were doing things that you were not cut out to do. This was what happened to me when I was promoted into a job that involved hours working on spreadsheets. I learned the knowledge and skills to be good enough at it, but I lacked the excitement for numbers and data so I was never going to love it. Our strengths are important because:

- They are the real us. What's the point in going against the grain of who we are when we can thrive by being more of who we actually are?
- They make us confident because they are us at our best – they're the things we're naturally good at.
- We can let go of the idea that we should be different in some way.

Living a life where we spend most of our time playing to our strengths is the only way to be satisfied.

And the big thing about strengths is they mean we get to live our life, not somebody else's!

– *The Strengths Book,*
Sally Bibb

THE HAPPINESS FORMULA

What does Coca-Cola have to do with happiness? At first glance, the relationship may not be very clear but, throughout the history of the brand, hundreds of clues help us understand how these two concepts came together – Coca-Cola and happiness – and how their blending produced the perfect symbiosis with clear benefits for the business and people involved.

The mythical formula of Coca-Cola, protected in unassailable safes and known only to a handful of people in the world, is most likely essential to keep Coca-Cola at the top of the list of those brands most admired worldwide. But the true keys to its success do not solely spring from its product, its bottle or even its label. The secret lies in what the brand has been transmitting to people over the years: a brand that continually invites us to look at the bright side of things so that we live happier lives. A philosophy that helps us understand some key features on how a simple refreshing drink leads to happiness.

The secret to success lies in maintaining a unique and strong brand identity.

– La Marca de la Felicidad,
Felix Muñoz

THE CHINESE CHALLENGE

From a historical perspective, relations between Latin America and China as economic blocs are taking their first steps. This implies that there are still many challenges but also many opportunities along the way. Latin American companies doing business with China are the experimental voice and they have told us so. China is a difficult market demanding long-term investments. But once a company gains access, it can enjoy juicy returns.

Therefore, the reasons why Latin American companies have not yet made the leap to China are not from a lack of opportunity or that the Chinese market does not need Latin American products. The reasons are more related to the lack of knowledge relating to China, the complexity of its market and the customary way we conduct business with our traditional partners. Why change if we are so accustomed to them? A good reason to do so is that the world is changing and that opportunities are changing with it.

It's important to understand the markets you operate in and educate yourself before jumping into new ones.

– *América Latina en China,*
Juan Antonio Fernández,
Javier Cuñat & María Puyuelo

THE PERFECT STATE

To avoid chaos, you need to know where you are going, and you need to be conscious of your decisions, your thinking and your focus. You may find yourself in a loop where you are continuously optimizing the decision-making process. Take a deep breath and inhale the air of chaos. Regardless of how we try to add mindfulness, deceleration and spirituality to our lives, the speed of change and the infinite revolution will not stop. The universe will continue to expand and the sun will shoot ahead at an ever-increasing speed. You cannot neglect speed, but you must respect it.

Entrepreneurs and businesses should invest in speed. Regardless of how much you focus, what you are good at or what you like, you need to invest in speed. Not big data, but the right data – for you, for everyone, in the right amount and at the right time. And make it fast! Today you need it all and, ideally, as technology has progressed, the information should be available to us before we even realize that we have a need for it.

As speed increases, frustration inevitably mounts with the realization that there is always a better decision that can be made. We fail fast, learn fast, fix fast.

– *Wild Knowledge,*
Anders Indset

Learn to value every good step you take and to love decisions that help you move in one direction.

HERITAGE AND FAMILY

In a family business, everyone shares the goal of earning money in an ethical and sustainable way. Perhaps the only discrepancy that may arise is what to do with the revenues and the surplus, meaning how much should be put aside for future growth and how much should be disbursed in dividends. In the patrimonial domain, numerous objectives take place, at least several for each owner of the estate, which may breed conflicting forces, sometimes limiting the decision-making process.

The management of the family estate is the combination of the family's assets, without the implication of joint management. On the contrary, one of the main focuses of family problems comes from the establishment of an 'all together at all times' policy, which easily results in tensions that have an inclination towards power games – ones that do not always take everyone's interests into consideration. Therefore, if we focus exclusively on estate management, without taking into account the members it serves, both investments and family health have no chance of succeeding.

Consider whether investments are more important than family foundations in order to maintain the management of family assets.

– *Gestión del Patrimonio Familiar,*
Borja Durán

LUXURY ONLINE

Luxury customers are getting younger. Generation X and Y shoppers, especially in Western countries, are single-person households until much later in life than were their parents. They have only their own wishes and desires to consider when they are spending. Research indicates that they are also more likely than their parents to have been exposed to luxury early in their lives. What they have in common with their predecessors, however, is that they expect their time and money to be valued by the brands they invest in. As we pointed out earlier, the post-recession consumer, especially in established economies, is looking for luxury that expresses sophistication. They desire something that is not for everyone.

Keeping these demographic changes in mind, we believe that brands must also consider a second development shaping the market: the near ubiquity of personal computers, tablets and smartphones among luxury consumers. They were able to afford the devices before anyone else and have consequently moulded their lives around them.

– Rethinking Luxury,
Martin C. Wittig,
Fabian Sommerrock,
Philip Beil & Markus Albers

Brands will have to offer more than a directory of online shops.

GLOBAL TECHNOLOGY

There has been a globalization peak during the past several hundred years, and companies have evolved from being local to regional, national, multinational and fully global. We have also seen an enormous increase in mergers and acquisitions activities in the past decades, creating larger and even more global companies. There are more strategic alliances with customers, suppliers and even competitors. The same pattern can be identified among customers strengthening their buying power. This trend is, of course, forced and enabled by the explosion of improved communication technologies, but also by education, freedom and demographics. Instead of economic imperialism, we see how companies start to practise economic diplomacy, realizing that it is vital to adapt to different cultures. The creation of global marketplaces is also generating highly segmented global bodies of potential customers. We see more and more specialized clusters. No one could have predicted the speed with which Google became a global company. Would it have become market leader if it had only focused on the US market? Globalization is not just a business phenomenon. It is an evolution bringing individuals, organizations, nations and cultures together.

Every organization is today taking the potential effects of globalization into account.

– *Surviving the Techstorm,*
Nicklas Bergman

HUMAN CITY

Today, more than half of all humans live in a city. By mid-century that number will exceed 70%. Our destiny has millions of us packed tightly into a dense maze of manufactured infrastructure. Cities have generally served humanity relatively well, lifting billions out of poverty and making possible an array of conveniences, from running water to high-speed internet. Cities generate most of the world's GDP. They are becoming the new centres of power, increasingly drawing it away from national governments. Without a doubt, the future belongs to cities.

We've pounded our earth with increasing speed and scale to mine the fuels to power our urban marvels. We've pushed our natural ecosystem beyond its capacity to feed the growing billions of urbanites. Toxic chemicals and waste kill millions of us every year.

Since we created this mess in cities, we're going to fix it in cities.

We must make people again the central context of our future city planning efforts. How different would cities look and function today had we insisted on building cars and the attendant infrastructure around human-centred cities, and not the other way around?

Technological solutions alone won't solve the world's problems.

– Dr Jonathan Reichental
for *Dialogue*

CATALYST FOR INNOVATION

Over the past 30 years or more, demographic changes, capital investment and open markets created a golden age for Chinese manufacturing, foreign trade and export, real estate development and other businesses. However, the demographic bonus has been disappearing, overseas market demand has shrunk and return on capital investment has fallen, forcing China to find or develop new drivers of economic growth. In Wenzhou, a shop owner told me a vivid story: a factory owner who lived across the street from him one day jumped from his balcony to his death. It was a day the shop owner would never forget; he even marked it on his calendar. That factory owner who committed suicide in Wenzhou symbolized the pain of economic transformation in China.

The key to China's economic growth lies in innovation, in enabling entrepreneurs to use new technologies and new models to achieve business transformation through equity financing – the most important catalyst for innovation.

Pioneering entrepreneurs are digging the grave of traditional industries and blazing the trail toward a new order.

– *The JD.com Story,*
Li Zhigang

CHAMELEON LEADERS AND COMPANIES

A chameleon has a 360° visual field. Its eyes rotate independently from one another. If one sees a predator approaching, the other, at the same time, looks for an escape. Still, the feature that everybody knows the best is probably its ability to change colour. Its moods influence the way its skin varies in colour. Each change implies something different.

Being chameleonic has a lot to do with flexibility and empathy. If we assign someone these characteristics, we are describing a person capable of adjusting, changing and switching behaviours and habits according to the needs of the environment. This ability will probably guarantee success in any field. These tough fundamentals in the private sphere are no less relevant in the labour market. Like the reptile, the chameleon company has an extraordinary ability to monitor what happens in its environment. It is up-to-date and updated on everything occurring. It studies the context, knows the state of the market, and plans its short- and long-term strategies based on clear objectives. With this 360° panorama, the chameleon company considers all markets, not only its own, and, if necessary, can even tweak its business model because it does not fear change.

– *The Company Camaleón,*
Antonella Fayer & Jorge Salinas

> **The chameleon company considers all markets and can even tweak its business model because it does not fear change.**

MEANINGFUL LIFE

To many people, the initial attraction of mindfulness is often as a stress-reduction technique. The ability to clarify the mind and relax the body, as a way to relieve stress, is compelling. But I would go further and argue that this is an altogether too limited view of the potential value of mindfulness practice.

In a genuine effort to distance the secular practice of mindfulness from its original role in nearly all religions, secular trainers often forget that the core of mindfulness is the cultivation of the mind's potential. Beyond the popular emphasis on mindfulness as a purely psychological technique, at its root it is an ethical and spiritual practice. And, of course, by spiritual I don't mean religious. The ultimate aim of mindfulness practice is to assist you to live a more satisfying and personally meaningful life.

Mindfulness originates within a tradition that views it as a path to personal liberation.

– *The Mindfulness Book,*
Martyn Newman

RECOGNIZING INSIGHTS

Good insights come from very different sources. Insights required for communications usually come from quotes (yes, quotes) related to the subject you are investigating. Quotes are nothing more than insightful thoughts about life. They capture our minds because they reflect reality using an angle we had never thought of before. And they are free to be used and communicate ideas powerfully. Another great source of insights is popular proverbs. They encapsulate thoughts and beliefs that have survived for generations and are universally accepted as true.

They often transcend cultures and religions. If properly used, they can provide a great source of inspiration for creativity. Your agencies and their creative teams should also be a good source of insights. And if they're not, you should start worrying. Finally, another powerful way to generate insights is to create your own 'wise men' panel. This is not difficult and does not necessarily require money. People want to provide perspective and advice. They want to help you. You just need to announce the creation of an 'Advisory Board' for your brand or business and make some phone calls.

Trust your suppliers, customers and experts. They know best what works and what does not.

– MARTKeting,
Javier Sánchez Lamelas

BRAND REPUTATION

There are two types of brand visibility that tie in with a company's social networks: the brand visibility campaigns and reputation management. The former helps to make the brand name memorable to a given audience. They focus on promoting the name of your brand so that customers remember it, also remembering where they've seen it. Not so easy. How many times have you seen an ad, though really entertaining, which failed to anchor the name of the company it was for? Even a catchy ad can fail when it comes to brand recall.

The other focus of brand visibility is reputation management. It works by guaranteeing that the brand keeps a positive reputation in the market and minimizes negative publicity. It works like a marriage: the managers of the brand have to be prepared to engineer positive media coverage and, more importantly, sometimes control negative news. It can be difficult because no one expects negative publicity and a lot of teams are not ready to deal with it. The best teams have detailed crisis management plans, which describe how the organization must respond in said situation.

Consider creating a crisis management plan to deal with unexpected negative news.

– *Cómo Monetizar las Redes Sociales,*
Pedro Rojas & Maria Redondo

GREAT LEADERS

In business, people often talk about change as a process, with a beginning and an end. "We are in a reorganization, it will be done by the end of August, then we're good to go again." Forget about ever being done. Change is constant; what arises will pass.

Great leaders understand that they have been successful when they are no longer needed. The worst managers make sure the whole organization is totally dependent on their presence. They think of themselves as decision makers and thus believe they should be involved in every decision and control as much as possible. But the objective for any organization is to become efficient, and a manager who is self-centred will create the opposite. A great metaphor is parenthood. The objective of any parent is to foster a child's independence. At times, a child will be on the wrong track and need directing, but essentially parenting is about support and patience and no matter how scary it feels, eventually every parent has to let go.

Great leaders are like parents. They don't always know what's best for their organizations and sometimes they feel insecure and scared about letting go. But their ambition is to make their organization strong and to create independence.

– Yoga for Leaders,
Stefan Hyttfors

You want employees to bring engagement and creativity to work, not only a pair of hands.

REALITY CHECK

Some marketers speak of the 'irrational customer'. Peter Drucker said that there was no such thing. He stated that the marketer should assume that the customer is always rational, even though this reality may be far different from the marketer's.

True value, like quality, is up to the customer, not the marketer. This is critical because customers, or organizational buyers, don't purchase a product or service. They purchase satisfaction of a want or need. This means it is their value.

Some companies spend millions providing additions that they think represent more value and are appreciated by the customer. Unfortunately, the customer may not think that these represent value. To a teenage girl, value might be defined primarily by fashion. Comfort might come a poor second. To the same teenage girl's mother, value may be represented by durability. To her father, value might be defined by price. Drucker knew that each customer has their own reality. That's why it's so important to do the market research.

It's the customer's reality that counts.

– Dr William A. Cohen
for *Dialogue*

STRENGTHS OR WEAKNESSES

The concept of fighting against our so-called defects is something so ingrained in our social structures that we no longer question it.

However, the secret to success and happiness is to do more of what we do well and spend less time on what we do wrong. Because if we do more of what we do well, we grow and develop in all our abilities. On the contrary, if we focus on solving what we do poorly, we limit our possibilities, because what we do wrong will always be an uphill struggle. The most we can hope for is to be competent (which in my opinion is mediocre).

I invite you to reflect on this topic. How coherent is your life? Do you focus more on your strengths rather than your weaknesses? If you have children, do you focus more on their strengths than weaknesses?

These are key questions of success: the principle of coherence is fundamental.

To become outstanding, you not only need talent but a positive attitude towards studying and learning how to learn as well.

Spending more time on what you do well, and less time on what you don't, will lead to greater happiness.

– *Los Principios del Éxito Hoy,*
Mac Kroupensky

HIGH STANDARDS

Having to part ways with people who no longer make the grade is one of the reasons why it is difficult to keep the team of A-players you need to become and remain iconic. Another difficulty is the temptation to lower your standards in periods when it becomes hard to attract talent. For example, during the dotcom bubble at the end of the 1990s, many candidates who might otherwise have joined consulting firms went instead to internet companies. At the same time, the turnover rate of good people was very high. The consulting firms found themselves under great pressure to take on candidates who were not quite good enough, simply in order to meet demand. Those firms that succumbed to this temptation spent the next years dealing with the consequences. Within these companies, the B they had taken on risked becoming a slow-acting poison when the A players saw that they too could apparently get away with taking their foot off the gas. And so everyone lowered their standards. Even when the internet bubble burst, and talent was again thicker on the ground, these companies had to put a lot of time and effort into raising the bar back up to its old height.

Even a handful of people who turn out to be less suitable can bring down a whole organization.

– *Iconic,*
Xavier Bekaert, Gillis Jonk,
Jan Raes & Phebo Wibbens

SEEKING EFFICIENCY

The new adopted labour measures go beyond mere reform. They are committed to changing our labour system, the dynamism of labour relations and, ultimately, in the medium term, the possible generation of a work culture that's different from the one that preceded it – a model that is adapted to contemporary business realities and closer to the countries of the European sphere.

It is well known that the Spanish labour market is inefficient. Its institutions are incapable of meeting the needs of a modern economy that faces huge challenges from globalization and the rapid transformation of modes of production in an environment of intense technological development. There is a high degree of consensus in the diagnosis of the situation. A thorough reform of the current system, which guarantees, in the long term, the competence of companies and workers to face changes, has been necessary.

Successful labour reform should address the needs of workers and the issue of unemployment as well as the fluctuations of economic cycles.

– 100 Preguntas Sobre la Reforma Laboral, Iñigo Sagardoy

DEMOCRATIC CHALLENGE

Companies build relationships more directly with government and society through the production of social value. Hence, the idea here is not the same as the one of corporate governance. That is solving the company's problems, particularly those related to shareholders and those who manage the company to maximize economic benefits from the former. Rather, it is a vision that, while taking company dynamics into consideration, brings them closer to solving social problems and promoting a social and political order based on democratic values. And this, we think, can only be achieved if companies consider the production of economic value through the production of social value.

In this way, we understand the 'social value', and specifically the production of social value, as all kinds of activities that form the internal processes of the company, managers and workers considered as potential generators of social profits, and which contribute to the strengthening of civic practices and social participation in the immediate environment. A business proceeding of this type is only possible if such action generates and, at the same time, is based on democratic social values.

Creating social value enables you to have more of an impact on your target audience.

– Empresa y Sociedad.
Generación de valor social,
Agustín Llamas Mendoza

AGE OF AGING

We live in the Age of Aging, which means that more of us are living longer and 'getting old' at an older age. This is life's way of offering a dividend, a bonus of extra years to extend our presence and influence on our personal world. This is great news if you're one of those people intent on extending your life so you can get to the bottom of your bucket list, but on a macro basis, aging is impacting the world in unprecedented and pervasive ways that must be reckoned with. Despite an abundance of global population statistics and the inevitability of mortality, the world has been slow to acknowledge that global aging is reshaping our cultural, political and economic landscape in ways that are as irreversible as aging itself. It's as if we have our heads buried in the sands of time.

Some of the smartest minds in business and politics are choosing to be blind to global aging which, while vastly perplexing, can be logically explained. First, aging is fundamentally an unpleasant topic as it's associated with mortality, and it's human nature to abhor that which is unfavourable (death) and to embrace that which is favourable (life). Second, aging is about change, in the sense that it is a dynamic of life but also from the standpoint that doing something about global aging will require changing something.

– *Getting Better with Age,*
Peter Hubbell

Even though change is a variable, we prefer to treat it as a constant.

BE
LIBERAL

The noblest word that the Spanish language contributed to the universal political vocabulary must be 'liberal'; a word written in many languages just as it is in Spanish. However, at the extreme opposite, our least noble contribution to the universal political vocabulary might be 'guerrilla'.

What does 'liberal' mean? Perhaps we must begin by admitting that, after more than 200 years, the meaning of the word has been broadened, adapting to new ages and encompassing ideas that were not explicit at its birth, back in Cádiz in 1810. At the same time, I have the feeling that the word 'liberal' has matured like a good wine; it has been improving with the passage of time. So much so that its enemies, seeing that in the present day it is not easy to attack those whose main creed is to defend freedom, have had to resort to a new term – neoliberal – to carry all their criticism of liberalism. Calling someone liberal today is a praise. A liberal's open attitude is a positive value and, along with tolerance, show's someone's willingness to understand others.

The meaning of the word 'liberal' has changed to become a compliment.

– Ideas en Libertad,
Carlos Espinosa de los Monteros

RIGHT POSTURE

'Right shooting results in a true hit' (*seicha seichu*) means that you have to face the target with a pure state of mind and correct posture, and then hit the target. But the arrow can hit the target accidentally without the archer being in the right state of mind or having the correct posture, which is why you can fail even if the arrow hits the target. In Japanese, the word for posture is '*shisei*'. But *shisei* has a broader meaning than posture. *Shisei* describes not only an exterior appearance but also an interior intention and force, which is manifested in a visible shape.

Having the correct posture means to aim to express through your shooting the qualities of truth, goodness and beauty. These attributes are like the archetypes of Plato; they are intangibles, existent only in the world of ideas. Everyone can grasp their essences intellectually. The archer tries his best to manifest these qualities throughout the stages and journey of shooting. Those who look at the performance of a master archer can feel the expression of these ideal qualities.

Kyudo instructs us in the art of correct shooting; we must think about what is 'correct' management in business.

– *Target,*
Jérôme Chouchan

STATE OF FLOW

Every business and organization is like a river. When a river is flowing, it is full of vitality, vibrant and healthy. In this buoyant natural state, a river creates an ecosystem in which everything is interdependent. Interdependence is an important and desirable state of being. Most individuals and most businesses spend their lives oscillating between a state of dependency and independence, neither of which is effective. If a river gets blocked for any reason, then it stagnates and starts to smell quickly. Many businesses operate within a dynamic of dependency. They are in a dependent relationship with clients and other stakeholders, and they foster dependent relationships within the organization. Middle management is overly fearful of making decisions and owning responsibility, as they are too dependent on the level of management above them. Dependency is based on neediness and creates anxiety.

At the other end of the spectrum, many businesses operate from a dynamic of independence. They are distant and aloof from clients and other stakeholders and foster a culture in which individuals and teams operate as silos and do not communicate with each other.

The dynamic of interdependence is the nature of partnership.

– Business Alchemy,
Andrew Wallas

A TEAM SPORT

Resilient teams share the value of kindness. Being kind makes you approachable, easier to deal with and fosters mutual goodwill. More than this, the team does three specific things. First, they value and make time for reflection, on team dynamics as well as on the task, however hard the pressure; going slow to go fast.

Second, they understand the difference between adaptive and technical challenges in change. Much teamwork is technical and requires expertise. Adaptive situations, on the other hand, have no obvious expert solution. Resilient teams avoid the temptation of applying a technical quick fix to adaptive challenges, which always fail in the long run. Resilient teams are sceptical about quick fixes and are prepared to engage in debate and cope with the anxiety and frustration that adaptive solutions can engender.

And third, resilient teams are curious about new ideas wherever they are found. They are prone to explore, rather than reject new approaches, even if they challenge tried and tested team methods.

Does anyone remember Tom Peters' advice to hire nice, because you can't train nice?

– Kathleen King, John Higgins & Howell Schroeder for *Dialogue*

FEEDBACK LOOPS

In your day-to-day life you are experiencing feedback loops all the time and these give you a clue as to what to do next. When you talk to other people, you are usually scanning for signs of connection, understanding, resonance and so on. When you watch two people speaking, pay attention to how the listener will often nod their head or make sounds such as "uh huh". This is valuable feedback for the speaker.

To demonstrate our need for feedback, find someone to talk to and when they are speaking, keep your head perfectly still, do not make any gestures or sounds, keep your face completely expressionless and just look at them neutrally. Notice how this absence of feedback quickly causes the other person to become uncomfortable because they have nothing to respond to.

The next time you meet someone, be aware of the tone in their voice, their gestures, their energy shifts.

– *My 31 Practices,*
Alan Williams & Steve Payne

DEMOCRACY AND COMMUNITY

I do not believe in victimization. It's not productive to be consumed by the social debts left by past mismanagement or to obsess over past corruption. Neither do I believe that it is necessary to reject those realities. The independent justice will judge on these issues. We Argentinians have to assume the level of responsibility corresponding to the achievements we proposed. And this responsibility breathes future.

A government does not make a change: a national community does when it abandons the convenience of complaining and embraces the excitement of development. We know that it is a demanding position, but also one yielding the greatest rewards. Many positive emotions travel the path of growth. They arise when the inhabitants of a country make an active use of the freedoms of democracy with conviction. Democracy should never be taken for granted or definitively be predictable. Democracy implies a path of constant and ambitious construction. The law and the institutions are the creations of a people who decided to give themselves a democratic government. When people build a nation, democracy becomes the permanent program of change that makes the nation possible.

It is possible to agree on diverse positions in pursuit of the good of democracy.

– *Ideas en Libertad,*
Mauricio Macri

SURPRISE AND MYSTERY

Surprisingly, surprise is something that is given relatively little attention in the construction of business communication.

Surprise is one of the 'big six' universal human emotions and so is something that we all appreciate in a good story as in life, as well as being part of serendipity.

Cinematically, just think of the "oh, so he's dead all along", "she's actually a man" or "he's actually his mother". In the lexicon of horror movies, there is a term for moment of heightened shock: 'chair-jumper' shots.

In what is described as the contrast effect, you should use surprise sparingly: no-one likes too many surprises and the pattern which the surprise is intended to disrupt then becomes too chaotic. The bizarre, it appears, is best remembered when located in the context of a normal storyline and when it suddenly departs from the expected. For maximum benefit, the research suggests that events should also violate just one fundamental principle.

So ponder how to use surprise to galvanise your gathering into action.

Ponder how to use a surprise to galvanize your gathering into action.

– *The Storytelling Book,*
Anthony Tasgal

MISSIONS AND RESPONSIBILITIES

The goal of an enterprise is to create value for its customers and achieve business success. Competition in the business world is in essence about company management. The missions and responsibilities of managers at all levels are to live and pass on the corporate culture and core values; take the corporate culture and core values as their central focus; manage value creation, assessments and distribution; and lead their teams to continuously create value for customers, thereby achieving business success and long-term survival for the company.

The basic responsibilities of managers include improving productivity, giving employees a sense of accomplishment, and creating a promising future for the company by working actively and responsibly based on corporate requirements. How well a manager fulfills these three responsibilities will determine to what extent he or she is accepted by subordinates.

Managers' top priority is to set the correct direction. They must focus on the most important issue and the key factors that influence it, and properly control the pace and flexibility required to achieve goals.

Strategic thinking in a manager means having a global view that allows a clear understanding of short-term and long-term interests.

– *Dedication,*
Huang Weiwei

CREATIVE ENGINEERING

Sometimes when young companies with rapid sales growth reach a stage of maturity, they turn to more aggressive accounting policies that allow them to (fictitiously) maintain the organic growth rates assumed in the past. At other times, the management teams of listed companies offer the stock market a guidance of results (sales and profits per share) either on a quarterly or annual basis.

The pressure executives are subjected to in an effort to reach these figures is enormous, especially since the arrival of hedge funds, which with their leveraged strategies are able to create high volatility in the stock price when the company does not reach targeted results. Faced with this pressure, the team can adopt aggressive policies of revenue appreciation to reach price guidance, or simply reach the midpoint of the estimates of analysts covering the company. However, the reasons may be even more pernicious. Thus, if the executives believe that they may miss the analysts' estimates, which can cause a breakdown in the stock price, which in turn affects the value of their stock options or various remunerations, they can take advantage of aggressive revenue appreciation in order to 'save the year' at the expense of reducing future volume of incomes and benefits.

We must avoid fictitious maintenance of financial growth purely for the sake of meeting expectations.

– *Ingeniería Financeria,*
Ignacio de la Torre

PERSONAL PURPOSE

Your personal purpose is your raison d'être – your reason for being. It is what gives your life meaning, direction and inspiration. It is a deep sense of knowing what is true for you which, if you follow, will ensure that you flourish, be the best version of yourself and fulfil your potential. I believe that probably the most significant part of your life's journey is to discover what your purpose is. Your life's joy is to live it.

To discover your purpose requires an open mind and a genuine willingness focused on peak experiences in your life. When you are on purpose you are at your best. When you are on purpose you are in flow. When you are on purpose you are inspired. The act of reflecting upon lifetime highlights and defining what they mean to you will bring together the key themes that are most precious to you such as making a difference, adding value and creating possibility. By continuing to dig deeper into why these are so important to you, you will learn the essence of your big 'why', which is at the heart of your purpose.

– Purpose,
Ben Renshaw

The starting point for relating to the world today is through the lens of purpose.

ENTREPRENEURIAL SPIRIT

Colonial entrepreneurs and intellectuals participated in the construction of the Mexican nation, particularly those whose example and inheritance had a heavy influence on the path taken during the post-independent period. The 18th century was the century of the great contemporary revolutions that marked the economic and cultural growth of the end of the colonial period. Entrepreneurs turned this period into a paradigm of wealth that sought to recover what they felt had been lost through several generations in the 19th century. The legacy of the 18th century is also illustrated in the field of art and culture during the brilliant Bourbons and the mindset derived from liberal ideas that, along with the lessons of the French Revolution, guided the political reforms of this independent period. The historical literature of the Bourbon period covered the first changes suffered from the insertion of the New Spain in the international market, which was intensified by the rich guild of miners and the consulates of Mexico and Veracruz.

The 18th century was the century of the great contemporary revolutions that marked the economic and cultural growth of the end of the colonial period.

– 200 Emprendedores Mexicanos,
Leonor Ludlow

POTENTIAL INSIGHTS

Instant messaging provides many wonderful benefits, but what precisely is it? From a technological point of view, it is a form of communication software that has consistently proven to be superior to the alternative electronic means of communication. It combines the immediacy of the telephone with the simultaneity of email in an effective hybrid form.

Before instant messaging became commonplace, the range of functional possibilities it offered seemed unimaginable. This was because, along with the ceaseless reinvention and perfection of instant messaging technology, it was able to move offline into the spheres of voice messaging, email, net conferencing and SMS – a complete one-stop shop. In addition to these benefits, this compilation of functions could be organized, easily assimilated and learned by users.

Instant messaging was created by three young men from Israel. Initially, they had simply planned to create a communication tool for their own use, but their insight destined the small program for greatness. Eventually it became a widely-used online communication tool.

– *Ma Huateng & Tencent,*
Leng Hu

What started as a simple way to communicate between three people became a worldwide phenonmenon.

FINANCIALLY SPECIFIC

In order to gain real clarity over what you want your future to look like, ask yourself a few simple questions:

- If you no longer needed to work, what would you do with your day?
- What are your basic requirements, what are the 'nice to haves', and what would you like to do in your dreams?
- If money were no object, what would you do with your time?
- Is there anything you really want to do that you have never done?

Dare to dream. Go on. Try to imagine the future in daily terms. How would you like to spend your time? Of course, this will be somewhat circular. You may dream of a life that is out of reach. Actually, the opposite is often the case – many people envisage a life constrained by what they think they can afford.

Be sensible. What are the things that would make you happy?

– *The Financial Wellbeing Book,*
Chris Budd

SMART FEEDBACK

Dialoguing with an open mind, without fear of conflict, far from separating the team, brings members closer by inviting them to communicate, give and receive feedback in an open manner, thus allowing for decisions to be made and problems solved.

Besides, both trust and proper management of conflicts are essential for achieving the true commitment of all team members. There is a form of commitment that people reach when everything has been discussed and clarified, and ambiguity of all kind is avoided.

Without this commitment, assuming our responsibility both individually and collectively becomes complex, and the results would yield a lowering of excellence and compliance standards. A team with responsible and co-responsible members is a team that constantly challenges itself to excel. This, added to the attention in the common objective above individual interests or status, will make it possible to achieve extraordinary results. Have you noticed? Everything starts with trust. It is the base of the pyramid of high-performance teams, of companies that grow and aim for excellence.

– *Smart Feedback,*
Jane Rodríguez del Tronco,
Rosa Rodríguez del Tronco
& Noemí Vico García

Create an environment of trust to encourage open dialogue and feedback.

COURAGEOUS ANALYST

An analyst needs at times to be prepared to challenge the status quo by boldly expressing original thinking and going to the mat to defend those ideas. Yesmanship may be an easier approach for an analyst who wants to retain his credibility and his reputation for objectivity. Respectfully but persistently sticking to a well-substantiated analytic conclusion that may not be entirely popular with a company's leadership requires courage. Analysts should have such courage, trusting their intellect and their employability.

Courage is not universally defined. It differs by culture. Assuming a respectful but challenging position with a decision-maker may be common and perfectly acceptable in some cultures, whereas in others exactly the same behaviour may be considered bravery.

When hiring strategic analysts, look for those who are willing to speak up when they need to.

– *The Strategic Analysis Cycle – Handbook,*
Erik Elgersma

PUSH AND PULL

The world has become much more transparent in recent years. Before, you could turn a 'decent' product into a commercial success through clever marketing. Nowadays it's impossible to claim product benefits that are not totally true, or even not entirely true. And it's hardly any use to add a beautiful cosmetic layer when there is no relation to what's on the inside. Consumers look through that easily, helped by an abundance of possibilities to share experiences. Because of that, the effectiveness of traditional push strategies is diminishing rapidly.

Previously, 'lean back' media were dominant; predominantly TV and print. Now it's all about 'lean forward' media; the internet, social media, mobile. Limiting yourself to only transmitting messages doesn't really fit with media that consumers use actively. 'Lean forward' media implies establishing a dialogue.

Technology helps consumers to make better informed and more rational decisions, and they are making use of this. Customers go through a significant part of the buying cycle before they contact the bank or insurance firm.

Several developments have led to the diminishing effect of push and an increasing significance of pull.

– *Reinventing Customer Engagement,*
Roger Peverelli & Reggy de Feniks

VARGAS LLOSA

Nothing is more suspicious than writers relinquishing before politics. It is not that their works predict moral deficiencies, but that they will invite stolidity. And they will not matter. Nothing in life is outside politics. And only politics is capable of similar transversality. Literature and politics are different forms of expression, but both require a powerful mind, and both seek to persuade and conquer. Literature, the realist way Vargas Llosa practises it, presumes a suspension of disbelief. In its best embodiment, politics as well. That is the engaging lesson in *The Fish in the Water*, one of the greatest books in political literature ever written.

There are liberals who fawn on and celebrate the collective to a point that they themselves stop believing in it. Their main argument and purpose may be the individual, but their confidence and faith in the people are not far from those of Marxists or nationalists. I'm used to saying: "What a great liberal I'd be if only I had a town."

While many choose to ignore it, there is little in life outside politics.

– Ideas en Libertad,
Arcadi Espada

NOTHING IS BETTER

Nothing is better – you are so busy, so full, magnetically attracting all sorts of things into the gaps in your days, without conscious choice. A leader who looks flustered and stressed sends a visual message that is far from calm and effective. This Impact Note waves the banner for 'simply nothing', which might just be the best choice you could make. Having impact is not about filling every single moment with action… your presence communicates composed, purposeful action.

Today, you are surrounded by more data-minutiae than has ever existed before. Emails, texts, social media feeds, alluring online games and apps, meetings, calls, alerts and then there is work to be done, information to read, research to be sought, conversations to be had, people to be influenced.

Finding and following your purpose and making your way through this forest of distractions is the challenge faced by everyone, but particularly by those at the top of organizations – and those with assistants who organize their diaries for 'maximum efficiency'. As you become busier, it is likely you will begin to let go of a proportion of your conscious choices about what you do and where you spend your time. It is almost inevitable, but not compulsory.

– *The Impact Book,*
Simon Tyler

Nothing could be where you reclaim overview, your focus, your intention and your power.

UNLOCKING YOUR CODE

Many great thinkers and creators have found that the best ideas are ones that are 'stolen and improved.' Feel free to steal as many ideas as you wish from what you have read here. Just imagine the improvement in sales performance globally if every salesperson everywhere adopted just one or two of the ideas we've learned about and moved their balance of intensity closer to what we now know is the 'sweet-spot' position. Think of it like tuning an old-fashioned radio, before the days of digital streaming. You hear the white noise and, as you turn the tuning dial, you hear the faint sounds of the channel you seek. You keep turning the dial and suddenly, there it is – a clear, strong signal. This is very much the same. It may take time, as you turn your inner dial, to find your own clear, strong signal. But it's there, transmitting. Your favourite spot on the dial awaits!

When we adopt some of the behaviours other people display we call it 'modelling'. Anyone reading this book can model. We know this because throughout your life you will have been modelling other people, knowingly or subconsciously. It's how we learn and grow.

Each of us has the capacity to show curiosity about someone or something.

– *The Salesperson's Secret Code,*
Ian Mills, Mark Ridley,
Ben Laker & Tim Chapman

SILENCE IS GOLDEN

Do you listen to the radio when you are alone? Or keep the TV on in the background when you cook? Why?

Tim Wilson and University of Virginia colleagues left volunteers aged 18–77 alone in an empty, silent room. Deprived of any distraction – not even paper and pens were allowed – the volunteers were left alone with their thoughts and their silences.

Most volunteers reported they were uncomfortable and almost all said they were bored.

Kicking it up a notch, researchers then asked volunteers about electric shocks. All agreed they would all pay to avoid an electric shock. Volunteers were then sent back into the room for fifteen minutes. Or, if they couldn't stand the silence any longer, they could push a button and self-administer an electric shock, after which they could leave the room.

Almost half the group pushed the button.

"We have this huge brain and it's stuffed full of pleasant memories, and we have the ability to construct fantasies and stories," said Wilson at the time of publication. "We really thought this [thinking time] was something people would like."

The fear we might get to know ourselves better keeps us chasing noise and distraction.

– Kirsten Levermore for *Dialogue*

EMERGENT MISTRUST

The problem is that common marketing and procurement practices are often inappropriate for extracting the value they need from agencies. This is a holistic problem insofar as it implicates changes necessary for marketing, procurement and agencies. The prevalent condition of mistrust and divergent interests between these three was not designed, it emerged over time. As one party has changed its approach, the other two have reacted and this has happened over and over again until we have reached something described as 'normal'. This means that if one party suddenly changes its approach, the other two won't automatically snap back to match that change and create the missing value all of a sudden. If your existing marketing, procurement and agencies triangle is tied up in the inefficient knots of mistrust, and defensive, protective, aggressive behaviours, it will require a great deal of thought and vision to bring about a high-trust, productive, value-driven triangle.

The solution to the problem isn't easy; it is likely to require a change of management strategy.

– How to Buy a Gorilla,
David Meikle

GROWING IN ADVERSITY

In Latin America, as in other economic regions, the ability of companies to overcome economic cycles, to adapt quickly to changes in their environment, such as the globalization of markets and, at the same time, to generate competitive advantages within their industries, is vital to remaining in existence through time. The adaptation of companies depends on implementing effective changes for each moment and context. These changes have to be made both at the level of business variables and organization. The relevant changes have to be strategic in nature, in case they must deeply modify a practice that is not compatible with new competitive circumstances.

The statistical analysis of the factors that improved the performance of Latin American companies throughout time indicates that changes in business strategies had more of an impact on the longevity and leadership of companies, in their respective industries, than changes in organizational configurations.

It does not always have to be this way. Other studies have shown that organizational variables can be as important, or even more transcendent, as changes in business strategies.

– La Estrategia de las Latinas,
José Delacerda-Gastélum

How does your company respond to economic cycles and implement change?

CORPORATE BEHAVIOUR

Every person of power who wants to become more powerful needs supporters – people that they know (or hope) they can bring with them when the moment comes for them to make their bid for power. Every would-be leader needs followers, after all. Simply making it plain that you have singled out a particular person of power as your personal favourite – the one that you would willingly follow into battle – counts for a great deal. At the very least this means that you will be a useful foot soldier (to stick with the military metaphor); someone that the person of power can count as a 'supporter'. This is crucial. The corporation has a very keen sense of the extent of support for executives seeking significant power. On occasions, the corporation chooses to ignore this and selects someone 'unpopular' – an oddball whom the corporation believes has the particular skills and abilities that are needed above all else at a dangerous juncture. In general, however, the corporation wants to feel confident that its new leaders have followers; that they will slot easily into place with a ready-made support base of their own.

Powerful masters need loyal followers.

– *Machiavellian Intelligence,*
Dr Mark Powell &
Jonathan Gifford

TRUE SURRENDER

Leaders are known to dislike the idea of surrender. I have to admit that I also used to see surrendering as 'giving up', or 'losing' to someone else, which isn't easy for someone who is extremely competitive. But that definition is a very different type of surrender, or rather, a different type of frequency altogether, where we see life as a battle; someone wins, someone loses, versus trying to look for win-win situations that create long-term balance.

Think about it: when you have a cold and you want to get better as quickly as possible, does it help to resist your cold and go on as if you are fine? Or is it better to accept you have a cold, crawl into bed and rest for a day or two? Which approach do you think will ensure a quicker recovery? That is what I mean when I talk about surrender. Being able to surrender to the moment and its accompanying circumstances will enable you to transform the situation into the direction of your desire much quicker and with greater ease.

Surrender is about more than acceptance alone. There is an element of peace and, most importantly, faith. In other words, having trust. Surrender is about admitting and being at peace with the fact that we cannot always be in control.

> **Once you start practising the art of surrendering, you will notice it is actually quite tangible.**

– BE,
Bahriye Goren-Gulek

WORK ENJOYMENT

For many people, work is the chief misfortune of their lives. For others, it is the greatest source of satisfaction. On what is it dependant that for some work is lived as a tragedy and for others as a gift? The majority might say that it depends on previous lived experiences and the current circumstances where one works. Psychologists, inversely, might state that the fact we feel one way or another would not depend so much on the circumstances of each work, but on our way of living it.

We may feel good or bad depending on whether we know how to love and take care of ourselves in the workplace. At this point, there may be people who question how they can feel good at work when the boss makes their life miserable, or their colleagues seem like enemies, or the workday lasts up to 12 hours or when, after all their efforts, their salary does not cover basic needs. I understand that for many it may seem a provocation to say that whether one feels good or bad comes down fundamentally to us.

Adjust your own attitude towards work for a happier experience.

– Trabajar sin Sufrir,
María Jesús Alava

WHAT'S WRONG

The prevailing work culture is just one thing that can hold us back from giving more positive than corrective feedback. As humans, we're hardwired to pay more attention to what's wrong or missing than to what's right. It's a survival mechanism we've evolved with and it shows up even now. Lost a five-pound note on your journey home? It'll bug you for much longer than the glow of finding another one down the back of the sofa. Resource loss – what's deficient or lacking – packs a bigger punch for us than does resource gain. This means that whereas identifying areas for improvement probably comes easily to us, we all need to work that little bit harder to spot what someone's actually doing well.

Another point about our wiring that affects our approach to feedback is that we all have biases and they're so deeply embedded that most of us are completely unaware of them. For example, we can attribute our own errors to a whole host of external factors, but when it comes to successes, well (obviously!) they're down to us; our skills combined with the huge effort we put in. Yet we tend to do the exact opposite when it comes to others' errors and successes: we put the former down to the individual's innate failings and dismiss their successes as mere flukes and luck.

– *The Feedback Book,*
Dawn Sillett

The key to treating people fairly is to sharpen your powers of observation.

GEN Z BRAINS AT WORK

The adaption of the Gen Z brain to learn in short, sharp bursts and take on quick-fire problem solving also seems to come with an inability to focus for any length of time or to apply considered analysis or evaluation to complex issues. According to Dr John Ratey, associate clinical professor of psychiatry at Harvard Medical School, the rewiring of the Gen Z brain through technology has resulted in "acquired attention deficit disorder". The endless bombardment of digital data, he says, means a low boredom threshold.

The Gen Z shortened attention span has significant implications for learning and development in schools, colleges and beyond. The eschewal of steady and patient extrapolation of meaning from information, together with a minimal investment in genuine, full-blooded relationships in favour of the virtual here and now comes with a set of limited and short-term horizons.

For Gen Z, executive education is the antithesis of time for reflection and contemplation of the world's bigger issues.

As Gen Z'ers nimbly navigate the modern world of easily-accessed and freely available information, they demand immediate results or they quickly move on.

Loyalty is a fragile and short-term commodity and is only as good as their last interaction.

– Helena Boschi for *Dialogue*

COLOURFUL LANGUAGE

Colour has many applications in the world of visual communications. From signifying certain traits, to making things more aesthetically pleasing, colour, when used correctly, can have a powerful impact.

When working with a full palette of colours (such as you would have at your disposal when using PowerPoint or any other presentation application) you have many options available to you. Certain colours have certain associations. Green in many situations would signify a positive – a green 'go' light for instance. Similarly, red can be seen as signifying heat or something dangerous or restrictive.

Common associations for each colour include:
- Red: Passion, strength, excitement
- Orange: Warmth, friendliness, spirituality, balance
- Yellow: Happiness, fun, cheer
- Green: Nature, environment, calm, "go!", envy
- Blue: Stability, royalty, authority, coldness
- Purple: Romanticism, mysticism, nobility, royalty
- Brown: Earthiness, warmth, nature, rusticity
- Black: Sophistication, power, modernity, darkness, evil
- White: Purity, innocence, truth, peace.

– The Visual Communications Book,
Mark Edwards

A thoughtful use of colour will also ensure certain elements of your design stand out.

WORK STRESSORS

Work gives us meaning and a sense of purpose and achievement. It gets us up in the morning and provides structure and routine. It helps to define who we are and the work persona that transcends from this. But we can also lose ourselves in our jobs and become work slaves, especially in a long-hours culture.

We form a 'psychological contract' at work; a mutual relationship between us, the worker and the organization. In exchange for the work we do, or outputs, we are rewarded with remuneration and benefits, or inputs. In theory, that's all it takes, but in reality the demands placed on us can be wholly disproportionate to our capacity to manage them.

Understaffing, business imperatives and tight deadlines all contribute to feeling overwhelmed. An equally distressing contrast exists when we are underworked, overqualified or our jobs lack the demands that we need to motivate us. Both being overwhelmed and underworked require affirmative action.

Can you help someone who's overworked?

– *The Crisis Book,*
Rick Hughes,
Andrew Kinder
& Cary Cooper

PERFECTION AND FREEDOM

Perfection, unattainable as it may be, nevertheless remains the most refined ideal of our aesthetic and moral culture. We are confronted by the paradox of perfection, an unattainable quality historically introduced as a powerful religious-moral proposal: "Be perfect like your Father." If we look at our experience of perfection: perfection is a limited experience. Almost exclusively aesthetic, with a strong religious connotation.

Freedom is never a complete fruit. Freedom is the result of a constellation of actions directed towards it and more or less achieving it. Behaving freely during difficult situations is an achievement that requires practice and dedication of the sort that is plagued with failures. During those failures, we see freedom shine as a conditioned spirit. One of the drawbacks of democracy – which is a prodigious sum of free, individual and collective actions – is that it never ends up deserving our total approval. Three cheers for democracy! It is very hard to constantly support democracies. It is extraordinarily difficult to be constantly fair, patient or generous. But all these virtues are indispensable for a good democrat to be genuine rather than a speaker of empty rhetoric.

– *Ideas en Libertad,*
Álvaro Pombo

Perfection may be unattainable, but we should still strive to be genuine.

BE MEMORABLE

Memorability is like the wrapping on a present or the packaging of a product. Great wrapping or packaging on a cheap product can make that cheap product look expensive and outstanding, while cheap wrapping on an expensive product cheapens the brand and reduces the perceived quality. Some wine makers realized this a few decades ago. By sprucing up the label and adding some gold trim, they were able to increase the price of their bottled wine by significant percentages.

How can you turn your simple, applicable phrase or sentence and make it impossible to forget? Can you wrap your sentence in alliteration, turn it into an acronym, or make it rhyme? Can you empower your message and make it even more memorable with music, a picture or a graphical image?

For example, advertisers often turn their phrases into sing-along jingles. The music and the rhyming don't say anything in and of themselves, and serve no purpose other than making the message memorable. These songs lodge themselves in your memory, and you can probably repeat common ad jingles that you've heard on the radio or TV with little-to-no prompting.

Empower your message to be memorable.

– Be A Mindsetter,
Michael Gobran, William
Greenwald & Derek Roberts

START WITH DATA

Purpose is where everything begins in an organization. This is not a plan, or a strategic goal, but the overreaching higher ideal that guides efforts and choices made by the teams within it. It defines why the organization exists in the world and stays true to its mission. It does not change over time, irrespective of turbulence or hardship. It informs every team's ambitions, wherever they are or with whatever they are trying to achieve – human resources, operations, sales or strategy, and across geographic boundaries. When building a data-driven culture, start with your significant others, not data. The organization I use as the example above has a noble social purpose that naturally spurs support. Charities all over the world achieve this, which is why people volunteer to work for them and donate money to their cause.

Achieving this kind of attachment to purpose at a commercial organization is more difficult. But successful organizations achieve an externally oriented purpose that informs the actions of their teams every day. This purpose is critical in the creation of a data-driven organization. Purpose becomes a handrail for data-driven discovery. Relying on yesterday's advantage will kill you tomorrow.

An external orientation is more important today for organizations than it has ever been.

– *Seeing Around Corners,*
Graham Hogg

OVERCOMING ADVERSITIES

Being resilient doesn't mean that a person does not experience difficulty or anguish. Emotional pain and sadness are common in people who have suffered great adversities or traumas in their lives. In fact, the road to resilience is probably paved with obstacles affecting our emotional state. Resilience is not a trait that people have or don't have. Resilience includes behaviours, thoughts and actions, which anyone can learn and develop.

We could see it as the ability of a person or group to continue planning future projects, despite destabilizing events and sometimes dangerous living conditions. Resilience is situated in a stream of positive and dynamic psychology for the promotion of mental health. The testimonies of many people who have lived through a traumatic situation, and confronted and learned from it, confirm that it is a reality.

In addition, they were able to continue to develop and live at an even higher level, as if the assumed or real trauma had disclosed a latent and unsuspected resource in those affected.

Resilience is the choice to move forward in the face of adversity.

– Resiliencia, Gestión de un Naufragio,
Pilar Gómez-Acebo

ORGANIZATIONAL ANTIBODIES

It's important to remember that the dominant organizational capabilities are present for a reason: to maintain the current trajectory. When an organization thinks about changing its trajectory, it usually does this by establishing a set of change initiatives. These might include creating a new business unit, launching a new product, entering a new market, introducing a new distribution channel, acquiring a competitor, implementing a new IT platform, reengineering processes or moving production to a lower-cost geography. As we've previously discussed, organizations generally don't have a good track record in successfully undertaking these types of initiative. One of the major reasons is that the influence of their current capabilities is either underestimated or ignored. The reality is that when a change initiative comes up against organizational capabilities that are not in line with the target trajectory, the initiative will fail – particularly if the influence of existing organizational capabilities is not addressed. In these situations, the organizational capabilities that contributed to past success often act as 'antibodies' to change.

When changing an organization's trajectory, it's highly likely that new and different capabilities will be required, and the influence of others may need to be reduced or 'retired'.

– *Beyond Default,*
David Trafford & Peter Boggis

Organizational capabilities exist for a reason.

FUTURE THINKING

The next few seconds are 99% predictable. That's why we don't refer to them as 'The Future' but reserve that epithet to more distant places. The future is the uncertainty at the point where the shortcomings of our senses need to be augmented by our thoughts. Our five senses are preoccupied with and designed for the present. Should you happen to hear voices from a long time ago or feel flavours from next week, you might be blessed with supernatural abilities but it might also be time to have your head examined.

Beyond the present, however, lie an infinite amount of possibilities. What's around the corner down the street? What will the weather be like tomorrow? What am I going to do next weekend? How will I celebrate my fiftieth birthday? When will I retire? This is a tiny snapshot of the world beyond the present. Being unable to see, hear, touch, smell or taste it, however, means that we have to rely on our brain's capacity to time travel.

When does the future begin?

– When the Future Begins,
Magnus Lindkvist

FEAR REHAB

The first step is to acknowledge that there is a problem. Too many senior executives are in denial about the shabby state of their organizational culture or they don't think it matters – yet we all know that culture eats strategy for breakfast.

The second step is to get fear and lethargy out and excitement and ownership back into the system. If the problem is bad behaviour, leaders need to manage themselves better. They also need to reward good behaviour, not just financial results – *Fortune*'s 'Manager of the Century' Jack Welch insists on a scorecard balancing individuals' performance with how well they lived cultural values.

Thirdly, if every individual feels valued as a human being, not just as a work cog, they will want to put in more effort for the good of all.

Fourthly, an external focus is critical. If we know what the market and customers want and we are aware of how our competition is doing, then energy is rightly directed towards pleasing customers more than our competition.

Lastly, develop a culture of learning. Better-educated people produce more wealth. So keep on learning after school is behind us. And, remember, it's impossible to change and grow without making mistakes.

Eradicate fear, increase productivity and also help work become a lot more fun.

– Liz Mellon for *Dialogue*

Drive fright out of the system.

DYNAMICS OF IDEAS

In nature, mutations happen in tiny units – they are the small shifts in the strands of DNA which often involve but a single atom. When the ape-men mutated quickly towards becoming human, it was because they frequently got isolated into small units, which then reconnected. Within human communities, a change is typically derived from a single idea in the head of a single person. The person is typically inspired by others, but it still happens in just one person. While development is all about co-operation, a 'collective idea' doesn't really exist.

Human beings are generally herd animals and adapt to each other – so if decisions are taken collectively, they are rarely innovative. In addition, people in large organizations are typically risk-averse – it is safer to swim with the tide than to go against it. Thus, the best way to create maximum creativity is to have a community divided into many small, autonomous groups or individuals.

Small units are best at dreaming up new ideas.

– *The Creative Society,*
Lars Tvede

PROACTIVE PARENTING

The proactive parenting method consists of directing and leading parents towards the desired end results in the education of their children, while recognizing and respecting their unique and individual nature. It's more a parental approach than a specific technique. Based on prevention rather than on solving problems after they have occurred, proactive parenting must always remain present in the background, ready to move to the foreground when circumstances require it.

Being a proactive parent implies preventing or limiting behavioural problems while transmitting the family's ethical and moral values to educate happy and healthy children. It consists of three pillars: discipline and set boundaries, flexible parental techniques and the feeling of trust and control.

When used together, these three pillars provide parents with useful and adaptable tools, based on chosen values and preferences, to guide their family. There are no magic cures or procedures nor doctrines that parents can learn by heart to incorporate into the education of their children. Proactive parents learn about their child's development, reflect on the values they want to integrate into their family and learn how to feel safe when educating their children about these values.

– *Cómo Educar Adolescentes con Valores,* Deanna Mason

In order to teach children your ethical and moral values, you need to live them.

CONSCIOUSLY GENUINE

How do you know you are being authentic? When you are being your true self, of course. But who is your true self? In fact, who are you anyway? Are you your body? Are you your mind? Are you your collection of experiences to date? Are you the roles you play in life? Are you the stories you hold about yourself inside your head? Or are you the stories other people hold about you in their heads? What do you think?

Many of us lead our lives as if we are our identity. Our identities come in all shapes and sizes but there is a strong pull for many of us to be drawn into identities of high social standing, high incomes and a sizeable collection of tangible items and experiences to prove our significance. In other words, we are drawn to the conventional 'success identity', but what is your authentic self-identity?

We are who we choose to be. We have inherent gifts and talents with which we were born, and we've acquired new skills and understandings along the way. Yet, we have a choice about how we show up in life each day and in every situation. The key is to do this consciously, so that you are being who you want to be.

Authentic means being genuine or real. Who is the real you, the genuine article?

– The Success Book,
Tim Johnson

UNDERPERFORMING TEAMS

Our studies show that high-performing teams excel at establishing and continuously revisiting their team culture: they are constantly fine-tuning the rules.

The underlying requirement for this behaviour is simply a few key norms.

Every team needs good norms, but where to focus? The research tells us that groups make better collective decisions when they have two characteristics: independent thought and diverse perspectives.

In fact, a team's emotional intelligence (EQ) is a better predictor of performance than IQ because teams with high EQ create an environment where more members feel comfortable speaking their minds.

To set your team up for success, focus on a few key norms around how you share information, how you then make decisions and how you handle conflict should disagreements arise.

– Derek Newberry, Mario Moussa & Madeline Boyer for *Dialogue*

The bad news is most teams underperform.

INFLUENTIAL PEOPLE

Whatever your walk of life, you invariably influence on a daily basis and you draw on your influencing skills to get people to agree to your point of view. Imagine a teacher who is an expert in their subject but fails to inspire and influence their students, or a website developer who creates technically brilliant new designs but doesn't have the communication and influencing skills necessary to persuade their client to implement the changes.

It's clearly time to change our mindset and view selling as a communication tool that influences others. Only then will you truly understand the immense value influencing can bring to your life and make an effort to strengthen your daily influential interactions. This is particularly important in today's digital age, where we're bombarded with more information than ever before – much to the detriment of human interaction. Given this information overload, the ability to communicate personalized and meaningful messages is crucial to differentiating yourself and increasing your level of influence. So, whenever possible, resist the temptation to send an email or text to ask someone to help you and remember to ask them in person instead.

We all influence others every day.

– *The Influence Book,*
Nicole Soames

REVIVAL OF CREATIVITY

The word 'creativity' (*kreativitet*) first appeared in Danish around 50 years ago in 1964. The English-language word, however, is substantially older, dating all the way back to the 17th century. Before 1940, however, the word was rarely used outside of a theological context, with words denoting genius or imagination instead being used to describe the phenomena to which the word 'creativity' today applies. As a result, there is a marked association between the themes of 19th century research into genius and today's discourse of creativity – with, however, a decisive difference.

Creativity is today seen as vital for the survival of the knowledge economy. Creative skills may be unevenly distributed, but it is deemed important for as many people as possible to have the opportunity to begin regarding themselves as creative. With this in mind, it is often asserted that creativity is not solely the domain of artists but is, rather, an economically valuable, shared, observable process that everyone can learn to master.

Creativity is today seen as vital for the survival of the knowledge economy.

– *In the Shower with Picasso,*
Christian Stadil & Lene Tanggaard

RUNNING FROM UNCERTAINTY

Decisiveness has a longstanding history as a desirable leadership attribute; indecisiveness an unwelcome trait. Being in a state of indecisiveness – not knowing what to do – was found, almost universally, by researchers Shelley Taylor and Peter Gollwitzer to induce a state of neurotic pessimism.

We all know people for whom the state of not knowing is almost unbearable and the quest for certainty imperative.

At this point, it would seem obvious that ill-informed decisions are likely to be made: the drive to quieten the emotions arising in the period being a rational response; the decision itself anything but.

What is often forgotten about decision-making is that a decision should be a choice between real alternatives. So it is during the period of uncertainty, then that we must seek these alternatives and ensure that, as far as is possible, they are feasible and viable.

If leadership teams are to deliver high-quality decisions, they must develop their capacity to deal with uncertainty and recognize that, for many, it's not a comfortable place.

Anxiety over not knowing leads to irrationality.

– Kate Cooper for *Dialogue*

RIGHT NOW

Traditional methods of managing tasks often rely on the idea of priority as the main way of deciding what to do. This is unsatisfactory. Priority is really a binary idea - that 'this' is the only thing in the world you should be doing right now.

I often see the old sliding scale idea of priority being used to decide the order in which tasks should be completed. That's fine for children whose homework tends to come at them like items on a conveyor belt. But modern information work is different. Instead of a conveyor belt, messages and tasks arrive out-of-order and attention skips between lots of different strands that run in parallel (and sometimes collide).

It is better to consider what can be done right now, based on the current situation. Out of all of the things that could be done, you should decide what should be done. If you can get into the habit of making this choice based on your situation, you'll be making a big leap from efficiency to effectiveness. It will help you to make better use of your time and respond appropriately when both free time and emergencies appear.

Your situation consists of at least one context; that is, an environment which allows certain things to be done.

– *The Productivity Habits,*
Ben Elijah

MOTIVATIONAL FACTORS

When external forces attempt to influence our motivation, it is normal to rebel against these forces. In this way, we understand that extrinsic motivation has very little effect on us, or has a negative effect. External factors attempt to create compliance. Because, if we're perfectly honest here, isn't that the purpose behind all managers' well-intended attempts to motivate us – to engender compliance?

To ensure we comply with company objectives, stand straight in line and do what they want us to do? Researchers claim that when you use compliance as a motivational tool, defiance will almost always be the response.

A compliance/defiance reaction is perhaps not too difficult to understand. When someone else tries to control us, to get us to do what they want us to do, instead of what we want to do, there is a pretty good chance we will react defiantly. The secret lies in helping employees to understand why they should want the same thing as the company.

What you need to do, quite simply, is to align the interests of the company with those of its employees.

– *The Human Way,*
Kelly Odell

THE
GENDER

The strong background in professional socialization that managers receive from their fathers explains, in part, women's identification with that of male role models. Female managers try to gain access to power and authority by identifying with men. It is a way to show their fathers that they have learned the lessons. They are not emulating their male colleagues. The question is profound and anchored in their personality structure. At first, this posture is positive if it stands out against the mother figure in order to achieve greater autonomy.

Women in positions of power, who model patriarchal qualities (discipline, effort and perseverance), usually succeed and climb to the top of organizations. However, this attitude can be harmful if the woman needs her father's or partner's approval to feel valued. Likewise, if the husband or father reflects a negative attitude, he can injure the woman's self-esteem and stifle her development. We have witnessed in many interviewees the strength of these identification models, as well as their co-workers' discomfort when they detect them without understanding this behaviour.

Choose to be influenced by positive role models, regardless of gender, without seeking their validation.

– *Coaching y Diversidad,*
Alicia Kaufmann

HUMANIZING A DIGITAL WORLD

One thing that has not changed since the dawn of time, no matter how big the technological advances have been, is the need for businesses and people to build relationships. People do business with those they know, like and trust. We were all once limited geographically; now we can profit financially, intellectually and emotionally from the worlds we create.

Although technology can break down barriers and entry to market, one thing will always remain constant and that is who we are as people. The dehumanizing of the way we communicate via templates and automation to connect to others is the equivalent of a warm comfort blanket that shields us from being public and personable.

When businesses look at the role of social media, it does not change the way we interact. It is, in essence, another method of communicating with a long-term goal of generating conversation, building rapport and interaction. However, it becomes lazy to think that all roads lead to Rome (aka Twitter, Facebook, LinkedIn and Google+).

Do we really think that the world of social media will help us lead better and more fulfilled lives?

– *The Content Revolution,*
Mark Masters

STUCKNESS PREDICAMENT

The ambience and culture of many organizations seems to encourage inertia – it is so difficult to get things done. This can provoke a sense of fatalism in many top executives. As one put it to me: "We can never change fast enough; let my successor deal with it!"

Senior executives in established enterprises can feel stuck, because the institution takes on a mind of its own and it seems impossible to shake it into a different direction. The organization takes on a web of perceived reality, which is woven into the very fabric of the enterprise; assumptions cannot be questioned and have now become givens, and the idea of calling them into question is no longer intelligible to colleagues.

In the face of disruptive change from new competitors and business models, senior executives feel powerless to respond. They feel stuck in the reality of their own business model and value networks, and rationalize to themselves that the new competitor is unthreatening, even when it begins to affect the company's own business model and value networks.

– Disruption Denial,
David Guillebaud

The Stuckness Predicament reinforces denial.

EQUAL RIGHTS

Gender parity is fundamental for a society and its prosperity. The development and appropriate use of half of the total available talent in the world must be linked to global growth, competitiveness and development of economies and businesses.

Numerous models and empirical studies have proclaimed that the improvement of gender equality promotes significant economic benefits, which vary according to the condition of the economic systems of countries and the specific challenges they face. Recent estimates suggest that economic gender parity could add an additional 240 million dollars to the GDP of the United Kingdom; 1,201 billion to the United States'; 526 million to Japan and 285 million to Germany.

According to the International Labour Organization, if the 90 countries in the sample equalled their gender parity with the fastest neighbouring country, the global GDP could rise up to 12 billion dollars by 2025. The female talent pool continues to be one of the resources of creation of economic value that is most underutilized. It is wasted by its lack of progress or untapped from the base.

Challenge your company to promote gender parity for a more balanced labour market.

– Oportunidades Iguales,
Mirian Izquierdo

BLURRED BOUNDARIES

As our lives have become busier, finding the right work-life balance for us as individuals has also become tougher. It is a moving target for a start, although usually there are underlying trends in our behaviour and outlook, which cannot be ignored. Technology has made our lives so much easier, faster and more personal. We can speak to people any time of the night or day, tell a whole group what we are up to at any minute and find out facts at the click of a button. We seemingly can't live without our smart phones, tablets, e-readers, portable computers and the rest.

The downside has yet to be fully explored or understood, as we also now struggle to switch off and be out of reach when work wants something. It turns us into completely reactive animals. We no longer spend the same amount of time thinking and analyzing whether things are actually good for us, as we are too busy reacting to the constant stream of incoming noise.

The state of our mental health is a balancing act.

– *The Age-Nostic Man,*
Michael Hogg

URGENCY

Urgency is needed to focus people and encourage them to give their best performance.

Ensuring that employees are very familiar with the key strategic projects selected by top management helps to build this sense of urgency. Employees know they cannot postpone their work and that they have to deliver on time.

Clear deadlines, fixed goals and knowledge of the importance – and benefits – of each strategic project are tools with which to infuse the entire organization, both management and staff, with urgency and focus. These techniques also provide the sense that things are moving faster, almost as if the tempo at which the company usually works is doubled or tripled. People work harder – and results are achieved more quickly.

One point to take into account – and a real warning for top management – is to impose the sense of urgency carefully. This is probably the most important risk of a focused organization: putting too much pressure for too long on the staff and the organization – what I refer to as aggressive focus – can bring amazing short-term results but in the long-term is not sustainable.

Creating a sense of urgency is a competitive advantage.

– Antonio Nieto-Rodriguez
for *Dialogue*

LOSS OF FACE

The notion of 'face' or *mianzi* in China is often referred to and a reference here is important. The idea of 'face' is disarmingly simple. It is about showing the right level of respect to others. No one likes to be embarrassed, especially in front of friends or colleagues and this is no less the case in China than anywhere else in the world. However, it is a bit easier to make a mistake in China due to the complexity of the culture and layers of meaning attached to so many things. In addition, people can take offence at things that Westerners shrug off as either unimportant or irrelevant. It is possible to step on a cultural or social 'landmine' without even knowing it has gone off, until you are refused another meeting or find people politely but permanently 'unavailable'. The simple rule is to be polite to everyone. It costs nothing and pays dividends.

It is also important to pay as much attention to what is not said as to what is. Reading between the lines is an art form in China and it is easy to make mistakes here too, on both sides. Be as precise and explicit about what you mean as possible, to avoid ambiguity. There is an assumption by most Chinese people, who might not have experienced a Western culture before, that you will be meaning something additional to your words when you speak.

– Inside the Middle Kingdom,
Jonathan Geldart

If you feel there may be something being left unsaid, there probably is.

IMPORTANT DECISIONS

It's virtually impossible to plan your career road because there are so many factors that you won't be able to influence. Impact those you can and be prepared to view everything else as an opportunity. If you've found yourself in a redundancy or other potentially negative situation, it might seem inconceivable to view it as an opportunity. However, there are thousands of people who have found themselves in an undesirable career situation and then ended up in a much better place. Staying positive needs a lot of effort, discipline and resolve. Ask someone you trust to help you. Where would Wimbledon tennis champion Andy Murray be without the faith and support of his team and fans?

Even if you can't plan the journey, it's important to have an idea of the destination: where in your life you want to be in three, five, or even 10 years. This is called a life plan and it's a really good idea to review this every year, perhaps on 1 January, in readiness for the year ahead.

Having proper goals that contribute to where you want to get to really works.

– It's Never Ok To Kiss The Interviewer, Jane Sunley

THE FUTURE OF WORK

The world is becoming polarized while opportunities are equalized. Meaning that there are going to be less and less middle grounds: middle class, average salary, etc. Lynda Gratton even predicts the disappearance of the mid-level manager. How does this translate? Those who are already above will be even higher, whereas those who are below, will remain so forever. The world will be shaped like an hourglass.

Luckily, there is another reality which softens the harshness of the one above. Each and every person on earth, thanks to new technologies which reach the remotest corners of the planet, as well as globalization and hyperconnectivity, will have at their disposal, because they will have to rely on themselves, the possibility of belonging to the triangle above. The country of birth, the family condition and the social environment one grows in, will no longer determine the future.

- Knowmads,
Raquel Roca

Are you ready for the hourglass not to bury you?

ACTIVE LISTENING

How do we communicate when we want to establish contact with another person or we want to sell something?

The classic mistake is that we start talking a lot about ourselves and our products and services. We go, as it were, into salesman mode. Funnily enough, most of us feel uncomfortable about it – but we do it anyway.

If you want to establish a good relationship, it is crucial that the focus of attention should be on your conversational partner. Focus should be shifted from "how can you help me?" to "how can I help you?"

When you give the other person your full attention and show that you are interested in them, the creation of a positive atmosphere is already well under way, and that is a good starting point for establishing a useful relationship.

To create a positive atmosphere, you will need to be able to handle a number of communicative disciplines such as questioning techniques, small talk and active listening.

Create a positive attitude and communicate with your conversation partner's interests in mind.

– *The Networking Book,*
Simone Andersen

CONSOLIDATING TASKS

Sometimes it may seem unnecessary to define the first step required to begin a task, but by defining the subsequent steps and not the first you will be none the wiser about where to actually begin.

Sometimes you may think that it is too much work to write out full sentences and end up formulating the task ambiguously. Although this saves time initially, when reviewing your list later you may find that you have no idea what the note means.

Do not fall into the trap of the abstract – formulate the details of the tasks concretely and thoroughly. Define them in such detail that you will be able to do them in one go, or at least during the course of a day. If you first have to do one thing and then another before you can check a to-do task off the list, then divide it into two separate tasks instead. Yes, you will have more to-do tasks and, yes, they will take slightly longer to write down, but on the other hand you will create a list that you can feel safe with. You will no longer have to remember steps and segments of each to-do task that are not on the to-do list.

Do not fall into the trap of abstraction – formulate the tasks concretely and in detail.

– *Super Structured,*
David Stiernholm

EXACT
TERMS

The idea of writing this *Business Dictionary* arose out of the invasion of American business terms and, worse, from the lack of precision in their use. We are clearly in favour of the development and enrichment of our language, and we simply think that there is already, in the majority of cases, a Spanish word that explains, or can explain, a desired concept. Using or adapting a Spanish word has the advantage that its spelling and pronunciation are accessible to everyone. We can then focus our efforts on its meaning and correct use. As scientists, we must make sure that our terms are accurate and not misleading, bearing in mind that those around us and the general public can also gain access.

The majority of our communications is with our countrymen. Even if, at first, they may not know exactly what they want to say, they will always suggest a 'lifeline' word before a word like 'greenmail'. With new realities, Americans look for new names or give new meanings to existing words. In our opinion, we must do the same.

Language is constantly evolving and we must be creative with it in order not to lose its richness.

– *Diccionario Empresarial,*
Marcelino Elosua

EVOKING CREATIVITY

Most of us, most of the time, create the future from the past. It is a predictable future. If we are brave, we may push the boundaries out a bit and create some 'stretch goals'. But, essentially, the future we imagine for ourselves is an extrapolation of what went on before. We create the future as a function of our previous experience: what worked and what did not work, our likes and dislikes, our strengths and weaknesses, our successes and failures. Unconscious processes also create needs that demand to be fulfilled. Parents, family and cultural background all play their part – all from the past. You have to be strong and courageous to do something different – and that is after you have given yourself permission even to imagine something different. The funny thing is, the people who are supposed to have our best interests at heart are the people who do the most to ensure that we conform. 'But, dear, we have always thought you would become a doctor, just like your father. Why would you ever want to be a footballer?' (Why indeed?)

So is there another way of creating the future? Ultimately, not really, because it is nigh on impossible to imagine something that has not yet had existence. The only question is whether you are willing to be constrained by the past.

Look beyond what is merely reasonable and scale the heights of the extraordinary.

– *Effective Modern Coaching,*
Myles Downey

WHERE IS PR GOING

Our skills as relationship builders using strategy, deep understanding of our audience and what positively influences them can take PR in an infinite number of directions, if we take care to develop both the art and the craft of our discipline. Communicating a point of view persuasively, amplifying it well, building trust that prompts an action, or changes behaviouror, creates community, or manages a crisis. It's all PR.

This is not to say that PR could or should do everything. PR is a complement to, but discernibly different from, marketing. Similarly, strategic PR is not strategic business consulting, though our disciplines work beautifully together to solve business issues. Moreover, while PR utilizes paid media more and more these days – it actually has done so since the 1950s – advertising agencies remain different, valuable and necessary.

The fundamental business and practice of PR is broad and flexible and more important than ever.

– The Art & Craft of PR,
Sandra Stahl

THE WAR FOR TALENT

Battle Plan #1: Talent is fleeting, attract it – People with in-demand skills are now flooded with targeted job opportunities online and, as soon as they see a new opportunity, they move on;

Battle Plan #2: Learning is agile, embrace it – Generation Z will find out what they need to find out. They know what they want to know. Old company courses won't cut it – your training should be experiential and practical, not theoretical;

Battle Plan #3: Networking is powerful, anticipate it – The next generation has access to an increased number of professional networks and is able to understand what is out there and to share information about companies like never before. Employees are much less likely to take a chance on companies than they once were;

Battle Plan #4: Labour is entrepreneurial, harness it – A culture of internal entrepreneurialism will benefit you long after the talent has moved on;

Battle Plan #5: Cultures are changing, accept it – The guiding principle of organizations should be to talk with the new generation, not about them. Hear what they say, identify what drives them.

Generation X are the offspring of the new dawn and they do things differently.

– Sharmla Chetty for *Dialogue*

CONSTANT CURIOSITY

Being constantly curious is a prerequisite of any successful and creative businessperson.

If you don't understand something, don't just gloss over it. Find out.

If you don't know how something works, find out.

If you don't know the meaning of a word, look it up.

If you can't remember everything, write it down.

Keep a notebook.

Be a mental magpie. Be on the lookout for interesting stimuli.

Practice serendipity.

The more you think, the more it appears that you are (apparently) 'in the right place at the right time'.

Inquisitiveness coupled with diligent recordkeeping is a powerful combination.

Look everything up and write everything down.

– *The Smart Thinking Book,*
Kevin Duncan

SMART CITIES

An intelligent city or a *smart city* is a physical space that uses technology to face the growing challenges cities are facing due to the impact of four macrotrends: globalization and sustainability of the economic system; demographic evolutions; the effect of globalization; and other transformations such as new collaborative economic models, open data, the limitation of energy resources and the use of renewable energy. The population is increasingly virtual and demands new forms of relationships and access to services everywhere, and through the most convenient channels. A city must be smarter to respond to its ever-smarter population. Cities are an ecosystem of people, companies, infrastructures, buildings, vehicles, devices, machines and more, that interact in a massive and continuous way which, without a doubt, must meet the high level of its citizens: a hyperconnected society hoping to enjoy effective, simple and modern solutions to improve the quality of life.

– Smart Cities,
Marieta del Rivero

Consider the smart aspects of your city that you take for granted and how you can engage with it.

STARTING AT
THE BOTTOM

Pressure can be overwhelming during the first stages of the transition to self-employment, but using it positively helps keep complacency at bay.

Facebook is the enemy and will gobble your time if you allow it to. Make it a lunchtime treat and save it for after work. Nothing that cannot wait is ever happening on social media.

Listen to criticism. If you have someone in your world willing to provide honest feedback, take it all on board and act on it. They are invaluable people to have, not the enemy. An iron chin is a part of the freelance starter pack and taking offence is futile.

Lead with your stylistic strengths and the rest will come with practice.

Do not be afraid to start again if you have a creative revelation, whether on an individual piece or entire portfolio.

Trends are discernible in the arts, but creative output with personality and individualism is timeless. Make the trends follow you.

Rejection is tough, but for every 20 knock-backs, there's a door slightly ajar for you to force open.

– Champagne and Wax Crayons,
Ben Tallon

WORDS AND EXPRESSIONS

Words may be our friends but they can also betray us, lie to us and conceal their past from us. If we are a bit more inquisitive about the words we surround ourselves with, it can open up new insights and opportunities.

From another perspective, words are a form of literary and mental heuristic – a practical problem-solving device. They are nuggets of history, deep-fried and spiced; all the more tasty if we know who sourced, cooked and prepared them.

Words can operate as heuristics in the sense that they become shortcuts, mental crutches that we rely on in the brain's pursuit of what Daniel Kahneman in *Thinking, Fast and Slow* calls 'cognitive ease'. In the same way that Kahneman (and others such as Gerd Gigerenzer, Director at the Max Planck Institute for Human Development in Berlin) emphasizes the importance of heuristics in saving the brain energy in decision-making, so words and ideas do not need to be freshly brought to the surface, explored and dissected every time we want to use them.

Let's force ourselves to dig deeper and uncover the hidden riches beneath.

– *The Inspiratorium,*
Anthony Tasgal

SMILE MODE

Dealing effectively with others has many secrets, which are extremely beneficial. One of the most important is the smile. Smiling is the opposite of a threat. It is a gesture that means the same in all cultures.

One of the most famous men in the business world in the United States was Dale Carnegie. He held six basic principles of personal communication. The first was to smile. It is a great sign of courtesy. But it would appear that this gesture has been erased from the face of Spanish business people.

Try yourself. Glance at the pages of the economic press, and you'll spot angry men and women. Let's continue with the test. The higher the level these men and women have reached, the angrier they look. Even constipated. Maybe success smothers them? The people who succeed in this country have a bad temper. They collect prizes and look as if they have been hit over the head with them. They are uptight. They do not smile. They must be thinking that the camera is stealing their soul or something along those line.

Try smiling and see what difference in makes to your mood and the attitudes of those around you.

– *Las Once Verdades de la Communicación,* Carlos Salas

SUPPLY AND DEMAND

For the project to succeed, these two numbers have to be the same.

This simple view of the world gets messed up by two factors. First of all, demand has a tendency to go up – for example, stakeholders may say, "Can we have more things?", "Can we have extra things?", "Can it do this?" or "I thought I was getting that as well." Alternatively, the total work may turn out to have been underestimated, meaning that there is more work than we have people available to do it.

And then we get the worst of both worlds, because as demand goes up, supply goes down. This happens when we don't have access to the resources we expected. Or when somebody was meant to join the project last Monday but there's a delay on her other project, which means we won't get her for another four weeks. Or when we thought we'd have somebody full time but they end up doing only two days per week. You know how it goes.

If these two numbers – supply and demand – get out of balance, the project starts to drift. If they stay out of balance, the project will crash and burn.

Project management can be thought of as a problem in supply and demand.

– The Project Management Book,
Fergus O'Connell

SUPERHEROINISM

It's hard to go into work every day knowing that the odds are stacked against you as a woman. You are facing a primarily male-dominated environment, with all the statistics about lack of advancement opportunities, unconscious or hidden discrimination and lower pay for doing the same job as a man. But at least you know the odds – so you know what you're working with.

You also know that the ability to bounce back when you face adversity is likely to be your biggest asset.

$$Endurance = \frac{(Resilience + Adaptability + Perseverance)}{Reserves}$$

It's a bit like running a marathon.

Resilience is key because we need recovery time for our lungs and muscles. We must also be adaptable, as constantly changing circumstances mean we won't bounce back in exactly the same shape and we need to be able to work just as well, or better, in our new form. We also need perseverance. This gives us the energy to keep going until we achieve our goals. Underpinning the whole equation is 'reserves'. If we are running on empty, the entire equation could crumble at the first hurdle.

Ditch the Wonder Woman complex.

– Liz Mellon for *Dialogue*

ACROSS THE VALUE DIVIDE

As is the case with beauty, value is in the eye of the beholder. You decide what you value. Society at large, our culture, the advertising that bombards your senses daily, and even your peers can try and influence you with regard to what you should and shouldn't value, but ultimately, it comes down to you. We should agree that it comes down to the customer – the buyer.

Some of the things that we value can be objectively measured. For the most 'cost' conscious buyer, a £100 saving is absolutely measurable; whereas, for the buyer who values 'quality', this is a much more subjective value. One person's high-quality product is another person's low-quality product.

As such, to really connect with a person's needs, you must understand what a prospective customer really values. So how do you go about understanding what it is that they value? You ask them.

– *The Smart Selling Book,*
Mark Edwards

Get explicit details on how the customer defines, recognizes and measures value.

CONCEPT OF IDENTITY

Identity has many guises. People ask at a party, "What do you do?" They try to place your accent and try to establish if you are married. Your sexuality. Your age. Your religion. Your wealth. Your place in society. All in order to find out something about who you are. And Identity has many close cousins: I, me, myself. Person, self, personality. Then there is the ever-present "I" in our speaking and thinking, which demands examination for it is this that we frequently relate to as the seat of our self. But it is not so simple, for identity is elusive both as a thing and as a concept.

As a concept, theologians and religious leaders of every persuasion, psychologists, neuroscientists, anthropologists and philosophers, to name a few categories of interested parties, have through many centuries spoken and written about it, often expounding very different ideas. But there is little that can be said with absolute certainty, for there is no scientific evidence for the self.

We have such a strong sense of our selves and our identity that we do not often question it or reflect upon it.

– *Enabling Genius,*
Myles Downey & The Enabling
Genius Project Team

METIS INTELLIGENCE

I had never heard of *metis* before, a particular form of intelligence, an alternative to logical reasoning that ancient Greeks used to resolve everyday practical problems. The possessor of *metis* was considered an ingenious, insightful individual with a fertile imagination. He had the intellectual acumen to concoct tricks with artisanal skills and manual dexterity to build ingenious traps to achieve his ends.

The *metis* doesn't approach a problem directly, but rather makes detours and prowls about. When faced with an adversary or a problem, he does so by continually changing perspective until he discovers a weak point to attack. He acts without thinking. Advertisers are considered ingenious, insightful and imaginative people. Their office has little to do with the linear intelligence of logic. It is pure *metis* intelligence. They are opportunists. They catch ideas on the fly, invent or steal them from any area of life. They reinterpret to convert them into useful baits for communications. Advertisers uses techniques to attract and seduce. What the Greek essayist, Plutarch, called *sophisma*, a clever technique, advertisements are traps created from inspiration to cunningly deceive.

It's not always possible to think your way out of a problem; sometimes you have to act.

– *Desorden,*
Daniel Solana

MAKING CHOICES

As we age and have other responsibilities, life can seem to grow more complicated. Later on, after the children are grown, unencumbered by as many outside forces, the workplace or familial and social duties, we can focus better than when we were younger. Doing something because you want to, not because you should or have to, has always been most enjoyable.

Being able to make choices gets better with age.

– *The Book That Gets Better with Age,*
Tim Love

WORKING DIGITALLY

Banks have historically been organized like old-fashioned manufacturing businesses. Raw materials (deposits) come in at one end of the factory, processing occurs (managing liquidity and capital), and finished products emerge at the other end (such as mortgages advanced to customers to buy houses). Teams of people were dedicated to each stage and largely didn't care about what happened in other parts of the plant. Until recently, automation of these processes was an ideal outcome for banks – like a car manufacturer pursuing a Henry-Ford-style manufacturing revolution, banks wanted to automate the steps in the process to get to the end quicker with less manual intervention. But fundamentally the process steps were the same, in the same order, just being done faster by machines instead of people. The result was always the same – the bank designed the product, it made the product, then it went looking for people to buy the product.

Things could not be any more different in a digital design world, where the desire is always to 'design from the screen down' with the 'user experience' and 'user interface' of critical importance.

– Naked Banking,
Stephen Hogg, Paul Riseborough
& Karolina Morys

The digital way of thinking is to prioritise customer-focused performance metrics.

POWERFUL LANGUAGE

Language is not innocent. Words contain a vast force that can be used to our advantage or can operate in the opposite direction causing a lot of damage. We believe that the way we talk (to ourselves and with others) very much determines the resulting outcome.

Throughout the day, from the time we get up until we go to bed, we are constantly talking. This is something we all have in common, no matter the activity, the career or the age. We spend the whole day talking with ourselves (i.e. thinking) or conversing with others. Since we dedicate so much time to this activity, it is interesting to pay attention to the types of conversations we have and how we perform them. And yet this is something we are not usually aware of.

We receive no type of training in this respect. We learn by trial and error, through the lessons that life throws at us, acquiring along the way habits that harm us, make us feel bad or hinder our ability to act.

Pay attention to the language you use with both yourself and others so you can use it to your advantage.

– *No es lo Mismo,*
Silvia Guarnieri &
Ortiz de Zárate

NEED FOR ATTENTION

Customers are emotional and unpredictable. Customers have different physical needs, but similar emotional ones. Customers want you to care about them and pay attention to them and be trustworthy in all you do. Then they will love you and help you succeed.

Customers will remember how they felt emotionally about your product or services, long after they have forgotten what those products or services were. These are called 'moments of truth'.

If you connect with a customer emotionally, they will be loyal to you and will promote your products and services to their friends and colleagues.

If you abuse their emotions, they will do all in their power to harm you – if they don't get positive attention, they have an unfulfilled hunger, which they will go elsewhere to sate.

If you genuinely give customers attention throughout their customer journey, they will repay you.

– *The Reputation Book* ,
Guy Arnold & Russell Wood

FUND RAISING

Crowdfunding is not a new phenomenon and has been around in different forms for a while. It developed from crowdsourcing, where people get together to solve problems. For example, there may be a need to find a new way of delivering a product to clients or to create a new design for a local skate park. The crowd helps to generate the ideas behind these initiatives. In a way, crowdfunding is an extension of crowdsourcing; only now the crowd adds money (funding) to a project. It offers solutions to project needs in all sorts of fields, from technology to zoos.

There has been a lot of talk about broken banking systems and the need for change, but change is often very slow. Maybe we are witnessing a shift as people turn away from the traditional forms of retail and commercial banking and seek a more ethical and transparent way of raising money. Peer-to-peer lending fits these criteria.

We are the audience, the creators and the judges of this stuff that's getting produced.

– Crowdfunding Intelligence,
Chris Buckingham

STORYTELLING FOR TECHIES

Forty-three. It's just a number. It only makes sense if it is placed in context: for example, the projected decrease in revenue, by percentage, in a key product line. Data is never enough on its own. People tend to make decisions based on stories about numbers rather than the numbers themselves.

This often requires leaders in technical roles, like Finance, to shift from merely conveying data-based information to a strong storytelling approach.

A quick rule of thumb is to utilise the Center for Narrative Coaching & Leadership iMAP tool:

i – Look for insight. What unique meaning and value can you add to a situation?

M – What are your one or two key Messages?

A – Who is the Audience, hearing your message?

P – What is the Purpose of your message? What would you like the audience to do with your message?

Turn data into stories so laypeople will hear you.

– David Drake for *Dialogue*

A COLLABORATIVE ENTERPRISE

The Collaborative Enterprise is an organization that consistently demonstrates the collective capabilities to collaborate internally as individuals and as groups and teams. It recognizes and works coherently and productively with all its shareholders and stakeholders. It engages with its community, within and outside their industry as part of an ecosystem of inputs, outputs, suppliers, customers, vendors and partners. It does so to face, in a productive and meaningful way, the complexities of the modern international, interconnected and interdependent marketplace.

Most certainly, there are companies that operate at higher levels of collaboration than others. Some are on the path to system-wide collaboration and others may be less operative but, nonetheless, are on the same journey. All companies operate with some level of collaboration and the great majority of today's executives view collaboration as a key strategic capability.

The Collaborative Enterprise is more than a Learning Organization.

– Enabling Collaboration,
Martin Echavarria

NEW LUXURY

Most of the known brands were created and developed by the founding families, who had time, patience and perspective. Today, the luxury industry has ceased to be in the hands of its founders, or the self-starter artisans, to be in anyone's hands. The most prominent luxury business groups are listed on the stock exchange and investment funds are partners with many of them.

They are the new owners of this industry. Still, we ponder whether this new ownership system allows the value of prestige to be effectively developed, or whether these new owners push these brand managers to think short-term, putting at risk the prospect of lasting values. The current financial and economic crisis carries an enormous magnitude and global reach. The luxury industry and its reality are affected today. This also impacts and acts as a catalyst for changing consumer behaviour and its search for new values. This crisis will impact the preferences of consumers of luxury products, something we anticipate today and will discover in the future. We can already glimpse that consumers will be more patient, astute and demanding.

– Secretos de Lujo,
María Eugenia Girón

Do you experience luxury only to own a product or to communicate to others what you own?

DEPTH MIND

Making better use of your Depth Mind is an important skill for creative thinkers.

Your Depth Mind is your subconscious. Once you have experienced an un-concealing – typically in a third place when you are quite relaxed and doing something else – then you can start to trust your Depth Mind to sort things out and generate solutions once you have 'briefed' it.

But this doesn't just happen automatically. You need to train your Depth Mind and you can do that in various ways:

- Be constantly curious.
- Practice serendipity (the more you think, the more it appears you are in 'the right place at the right time').
- Become a Mental Magpie (collect stimuli often and from odd places).
- Widen your span of relevance (many inventions were conceived by those working in other fields and, as the saying goes, chance favours the prepared mind).

Draw up a plan to deliberately expose your mind to some unusual non-work stimuli.

– The Ideas Book,
Kevin Duncan

OUT OF OFFICE

We live in the age of 'always on'. The relentless pace of the world means work integrates into our lives in different ways. Gone are the days when the whistle blows at five and office workers stream into the late afternoon as a single exodus out towards the suburbs.

We are now global and connected, and we work in new ways. To support that, we need a different kind of workplace. The lines are blurred between work and life; it's no longer a question of balance, but of integration. If we're able to work at home, we need to feel at home at work. Productive places that help us to work, rest and play in any way we choose, at any time, are not a thing of the future. They are already breathing new life not only into our relationship with work, but into the cities they inhabit.

As humans, we connect with our work and workplace in very specific ways, individually and collectively.

– Work Transformed,
BDG

HOW RIGHT YOU ARE

It is incredibly difficult for super-smart people to hear something with which they disagree, without proving that the other person is wrong. After all, if others disagree with us, we assume, because we are so smart, they must be wrong. They may not be stupid, they are just confused.

One of the super-smart scientists I worked with, Dr Jones, led R&D for a large corporation. The good news was that he was very honest. The bad news was that he was blunt. When people 'took him on' he almost always proved they were wrong and he made them feel embarrassed.

Jones was always right. Until he was wrong. Jones mistakenly supported one disastrous decision and reduced the market capitalization of the company by more than $10bn!

The scientists who worked for him said they had had doubts about the project, but never raised them. Why? Since Jones was convinced that this was the right thing to do, they assumed he must be correct. Even though they had doubts, they didn't want to risk being humiliated.

The higher up we move in leadership, the more destructive this habit may become.

– Marshall Goldsmith
for *Dialogue*

RECOGNIZING DECISIONS

People commonly use the notions of purpose and meaning to achieve orientation and to make decisions. What gives people meaning is expressed through their values. What gives people purpose is expressed through their intentions or cause. People orient themselves and make decisions based on their purpose and their values. Orientation is a form of inquiry that integrates an external perspective and an internal perspective.

People commonly use the notion of outcome to reference the result of an action that is valued by others and impact to reference the ramifications of an action that is valued by others. Therefore, outcomes align and bridge intentions and impacts.

People commonly use the notion of options to reference the various ways that they may decide. Our choices are really our options. For example, we can decide to choose option A or option B based on their advantages and disadvantages. Exploring options, making decisions and taking actions must be done in a timely manner so as to ensure we don't get disorientated.

People commonly use the notion of experiments (trial and error, tinkering, or tweaking) to reference the refinement of their orientation based on their decisions, actions and observations.

– *The Antifragility Edge,*
Sinan Si Alhir

Our questions are really our experiments.

COMMUNICATION TRENDS

Trend 1. The main challenge in this trend is to involve all the people making up the company with the company's objectives and strategy.

Trend 2. All members of the company work towards becoming brand ambassadors both internally and externally.

Trend 3. Multichannel communications place the employee in the centre to provide tools that ensure fluid and multidirectional communications.

Trend 4. Companies implement simple recognition initiatives to reap good results from them.

Trend 5. They generate relevant and useful content based on storytelling to move and provoke reactions in coworkers.

Trend 6. Omni-channel communications aim to ensure that information flows in all directions within the organization, to reach coworkers through the most appropriate channels.

Trend 7. The challenge is to reach all employees regardless of where they are located, what type of role they play and what their job entails.

Trend 8. Efforts are made to capture employees' attention, via surprises and emotions. To achieve this, the company designs broad audiovisual media campaigns.

Effective communication trends ensure employees feel included.

– Comunicar Para Transformar,
Custodia Cabanas &
Asunción Soriano

PROFILING EXECUTIVES

The logical model underpinning the preparation of an executive profile when predicting a company's next steps is:

- Data collected from a range of sources allows an executive to be profiled.
- An executive with a particular profile will behave in a particular predictable way when facing particular circumstances.
- The company led by this executive is a shadow of this executive; i.e., the executive facing particular circumstances will make their predictable call on the decisions to be taken at a company level.
- By implication: knowing the circumstances and the executive's profile allows predicting the company's next steps within a certain level of accuracy.

A word of warning should be given here. Assessing the intent of another company is much harder than assessing the other company's more tangible capabilities.

– The Strategic Analysis Cycle – Tool Book, Erik Elgersma

Profiling executives matters most when single executives make key decisions.

UNTRUSTED MACHINATIONS

To be a trusted team member, you need at least three qualities: mutual concern, a shared sense of vulnerability and faith in competence. Of these three crucial factors, mutual concern is the most fundamental – unless you are convinced your boss, colleague or supplier cares for your own wellbeing, you are unlikely to trust them.

In stark contrast, humans are unwilling to trust robots. This lack of faith in AI has potentially huge consequences for the next few decades. Like an ostensibly competent employee whom, for whatever reason, you do not trust, they are of limited utility. We risk investing billions to make robots with incredible processing power, but to whom we give only the most mundane of tasks.

The problem comes from empathy, or perceived lack of it. Humans are almost universally disinclined to credit machines with any notion of 'feeling'. The calculations made by an 'Ian' versus an 'IanBot' would be largely similar. Yet because Ian can feel for my team's plight and Ianbot cannot, we are much keener to take our chances with the human.

Our distrust in machines will limit their use for all time.

– Kurt Gray for *Dialogue*

COMMUNICATIONS DEVELOPMENT

The best way to ensure that your talent brand is clearly communicated in all your employee and recruitment materials is to conduct a communications audit. This is when you collect all the pieces of information currently in use by all departments and analyse them against a set of criteria.

And though it sounds incredibly daunting, don't be threatened by the idea of it. It's not something that will undermine the great job you are already doing as a communications professional. A communications audit will showcase the work you are doing and help you to prioritize the projects you want to focus on. If you are working on a branding or rebranding initiative, this is the perfect time to embark on a communications audit and tie the two activities together.

– The Talent Brand,
Jody Ordioni

Prioritize through a communications audit.

EFFORTLESS FLOW

For some, Not Doing may seem sheer madness. It does not conform to the mainstream values of success, nor does it reinforce common assumptions about achievement. To find our way on the path of Not Doing, often we have to hit our edge first, acknowledging that things have fallen apart. The old way of doing things is no longer possible. This means that our strategies for coping, like building our endurance, may be insufficient, not serving us well in our new context. When we can no longer cling to the river shore, we know that we need to let go and come to the centre.

Not Doing requires us to understand ourselves in relation to the other forces at play. We are not operating in a vacuum, where the only thing that moves objects is our effort. It is a way to engage with, tap into and benefit from our environment. It requires effortless adaption to the environment, like the river that wends its way from spring to ocean, or the snake that moves in response to the contours of its surroundings.

Not Doing follows the contours of space and the flow of the current.

– Not Doing,
Diana Renner & Steven D'Souza

RETIREMENT AS AN OPPORTUNITY

The five strategies of living after retirement are:

The Busiers: They like challenges and believe in the value of work. Being useful and fulfilling duties are their main objectives. Their time is spent on a selected task, which delimits its own space and, provided they achieve their goals, generates new stimuli.

The Enjoyers: For these retirees, activity and leisure go hand in hand. They consider retirement as an ideal time to satisfy their desires and embark on new, familiar or delayed activities. Sharing the same hedonistic dimension, they find their personal mix of interests, hobbies and pleasant moments.

The Restful: This predisposition includes those who, once retired, chose to restrict their obligations to rest and live relaxed, and those who, over the years, evolved from a more active retirement period towards this restful lifestyle.

The Explorers: They have the talent to adapt to the challenges of retirement innovating. They regard it as a genuine challenge to which they must respond by achieving greater personal integration. Retirement is a beneficial occasion to acquire new knowledge or skills.

The Unfocusers: Among their aims, they frequently appear to be busy 'doing something' or distracted.

– La Jubilación. Una Nueva Oportunidad, Bartolomé Freire

Have a think about your retirement strategy now and plan for your future.

UNLOCK SHARED VALUE

Markets are evolving and becoming more complex. Business activity continues to grow – exponentially when measured in terms of GDP per capita. However, the social and environmental consequences of business activities, both positive and negative, are typically either not considered or are an afterthought. As we look around at the wide range of social issues from healthy eating and online privacy to responsible lending and environmental stewardship, it is clear that politicians and regulators often struggle to keep up.

The way the world communicates is also changing. Social media is giving a louder and clearer voice to a broad range of stakeholders that are directly or indirectly impacted. Hiding behind a veil of secrecy and opacity is no longer an option for companies or for governments. Information travels at lightning speed and social media makes everyone a potential journalist. Companies have become more accountable, whether they like it or not – answering not only for what they achieve but for how they achieve it. The implications of heightened accountability extend beyond internal operations to affect suppliers, customers and consumers alike. All become cogs in a wheel that serves – or disserves – the community.

Pursuing a broader business purpose offers greater potential for positive differentiation.

– *Australia 2034,*
Nigel P. Andrade & Peter D. Munro

INNOVATION CULTURE

One habit that distinguishes Best Innovators is the balancing of emotion and fact – their obvious commitment to innovation culture and process excellence. Active management of this balance needs to be visible to business-unit heads and ultimately to the chief executive officer. How senior leaders respond to the innovators in their organization tells their team – as well as analysts and investors – most of what they need to know about the seriousness of the company's commitment to innovation.

A balanced foundation of emotion and fact – of culture and process – creates the conditions for making innovation repeatable and efficient. Most entrants in the Best Innovator competition – the winners and the rest – give themselves high marks for both fact and emotion. Consider, for instance, the typical responses to the culture questions: is your organization excited about innovation? Genuinely open to new ideas? Ready for change? Check, check and check. But we often see something different when we get past this self-assessment to a rigorous observation of the organization in action.

– Masters of Innovation,
Kai Engel, Violetka Dirlea
& Jochen Graff

What is culture? And how do the Best Innovators build it?

DIGITAL MARKETING

Selling something is very complicated. We compete hard against opponents who want the same: to conquer consumers is what will make them achieve their goals. It is not enough to have a good product. Though a necessary condition to be successful in the medium and long-term, it is not enough. The sudden emergence of telecommunications and of new information technologies is radically transforming a broad range of human activities. Technology has changed and, along with it, consumer demand. New communication tools give us a bidirectional and interactive pathway, where we can intervene and contribute. The era of brands, when television dictated what the brands were (what companies decided), is over. The brands from now on are what people want them to be.

Consumers have changed but most brands have not. They are still determined to spread unidirectional, impersonal and half-true (more untrue than true in many cases) information. This no longer works. The digital environment calls for a change in philosophy. Approaching people requires a different method. More respectful. Rewarding those who endorse you and persuading those who criticize you. A return to the era of conversations.

Don't rely too heavily on social media for digital marketing plans but embrace it as part of the conversation.

– *Marketing Digital que Funciona,*
Nacho Somalo

SHAREHOLDER VALUE

What can companies do to increase their stock price? This is the crucial question, but one that no one really has THE answer to. There is a saying: CEOs of publicly traded companies have two sets of customers – those who buy their products and those who buy their shares of stock. Since the market value of a company depends on supply and demand, how do CEOs convince investors to buy or hold their companies' shares rather than avoid or sell them?

Many investors rely heavily on the recommendations of stock analysts. Thus, many of the efforts by companies whose shares are traded in the world's leading stock markets are focused on impressing these analysts. Companies know that analysts can judge whether their stocks are worth the investment using any of the metrics we have discussed. So it is up to a company's leadership, in particular the CEO with the help of the CFO, to do the following:

1. Select the target metrics that they believe will best impress the analysts.
2. Set the magnitude of these targets.
3. Hit the numerical targets and highlight this accomplishment.

– Buy Low, Sell High,
Dr Philip Young

Investors look for companies to have what they call a 'growth story'.

KICK IDEAS AROUND

The word 'silo' comes from the Greek word *siros*, meaning 'corn pit'.

The meaning moved across to military missile silos, and then to systems and departments that work in isolation. Synonyms include 'ghettos', 'buckets' and 'tribes'.

Businesses should strive to prevent silos in the first place, or work hard to remove them.

Ever since civilized society began, we have felt the need to classify, categorize and specialize. This can make things more efficient and help to give the leaders in organizations a sense of confidence that all is well.

But it can also create a 'structural fog', with the full picture of where the organization is heading hidden from view.

Silos are rife in many modern institutions. They have the power to collapse companies and destabilize markets.

They blind and confuse, often making companies act in risky and damaging ways.

So, when it comes to devising appropriate strategies, putting everything in its so-called place isn't always such a bright idea.

Before drawing first thoughts together, make sure you visit all corners of the business.

– *The Smart Strategy Book,*
Kevin Duncan

SIX MEN OF STRATEGY

I keep six honest serving men,
They taught me all I knew,
Their names are What and Why and When,
And How and Where and Who.
Rudyard Kipling

And that's all you need. These are big questions and the result of asking them should be a fully integrated strategic plan. The best strategic results will come from a senior management team taking time to undertake a proper internal and external analysis and vigorously debate the strategic options available.

Take the questions seriously and answer each in depth, challenging each other at every step. Remember that, with any strategy, you are trying to build on the core competency of the organization – something that is unique and hard to copy and often embedded in the culture.

While building on this core, don't project past ideas into the future. Think creatively and spend time looking for the 'difference that will make the difference' – ideas often found at the periphery of your industry or even in different sectors.

Strategic thinking should never start with 'why?'

– Mark Procter for *Dialogue*

FINDING HOME

For those of us for whom home is place, nomadic life can be challenging. Letting go of places is difficult by definition. We long for the physical elements of home, the stretch of beach on which we played as children, the sounds of the neighbourhood where we grew up, the smells of our favourite foods. Still, just because home is place does not mean that you cannot make successful moves. Being aware of your geographical concept of home can help you devise strategies for approaching the different phases of the moving process.

When home is more feeling than place, you need first to clarify what that feeling consists of. Is it having a safe haven? Feeling loved and accepted for who you are? Having a sense of belonging? Being clear about the emotional dimensions of home will help you find ways to recreate that home wherever you are.

When home is people, start by determining what relationships are at the core of your concept of home. For expats, these relationships are often spread out geographically and over time – they are bonds from your past and your present, across all the places that matter to you. Clarity about the people who make home for you will guide you to find home wherever you are.

Which of the concepts of home – as place, as feeling, as people or a combination – seems to fit you best?

– *A Great Move,*
Katia Vlachos

THE BEST TREASURE

There are people capable of being happy, despite the fact that everything or almost everything has turned against them. It is the ultimate evidence, the most complex challenge: to infer the meaning of life when wishing to be closer to death. Those who face adverse situations which are difficult to confront, or face conflicts and acute personal crises, have a different understanding of life once, and if, they're able to overcome these challenges.

The power of personal interpretation means that situations that bring on the edge of suffering, pain, failure and loss, can be overcome by reframing them. Obviously, such a personal option cannot be improvised. It requires an important spiritual awareness to connect us with a dimension to which few are accustomed.

Happiness is not a treasure to be discovered or a divine gift only granted to a privileged few. Happiness, if it is a goal, is a task that is sometimes simple and bearable, sometimes arduous and complicated, and which depends to a large extent on how we decide to face the challenges of everyday life.

Our happiness is often dependent not on our circumstances but our perspective.

– El Desafío de la Felicidad,
Ignacio Alvaréz de Mon

WHAT HAPPENED?

We have naturally evolved and casually taken a giant step forward. The importance of the internet in our lives has uniquely passed down to the very bottom of Maslow's hierarchy of needs.

Sure, many new inventions have 'early adopters' who open up markets for the broader population (think of mobile phones).

But in this case, what was once a highly specialist pursuit and almost undercover skill among a few so called 'cyber gypsies', in the mid- to late-80s has not become a mass-market toy, gismo, gimmick and 'nice-to-have'. It has become a physiological necessity for the billions who now exist online.

In 20 years the internet has evolved from a business tool to an extension of man.

It has now become a characteristic of the normal functioning of our lives, just a tiny notch above the things without which would cause our demise: breathing, food, water and sleep, but on the same level as the physiological need for stability and sex.

Homo Sapiens has acquired a new dependency like never before.

– *Implosion,*
Andy Law

AVOIDING UNCERTAINTY

The future is hurtling towards us faster than ever before – in fact; it's already upon us. Moreover, it is full of uncertainty – of risk and, in the view of many, chaos.

The situations we experience are so different from what we've previously experienced; the information we struggle to digest so comprehensive, the risks we face so hard to foresee and avoid – harder than ever in a world where the improbable tends to occur with improbable frequency.

Times such as these demand active engagement; otherwise we will be swept in the wrong direction: backwards.

More than ever, we need to summon the guts it takes to act and make decisions. It is only then that we can pave the way towards security, and effectively address risk and uncertainty.

We create security by seeing opportunities where others see problems – by making decisions when others do not dare: we act, even though we, ourselves, are similarly uncertain about the outcome. We gain security through action.

In challenging times, the widely lauded character trait of being cautious is obviously often prevalent – we don't want to rock the boat, and we don't want to take any risks.

– Freestyle Decision Making,
Dr Mona Riabacke &
Dr Ari Riabacke

People who won't take risks are trying to preserve what they already have. People who take risks often wind up having more.

THE LIBERALS

Because of the healthy insistence on claiming a freer soci-ety as a principle, rather than maintaining the *status quo*, liberals – who postulate these ideals without even looking for geographical or historical references – are often labelled as idealists or theorists. We love imagining a freer society than the one we have. We constantly denounce all possible types of oppression. But when the time comes to making decisions and concrete proposals for change, we repeat the same chorus that the State must shrink so that the market can take its place.

It is thus that the practical man, though he may share liberal values, is the one who is forced to embrace far less liberal proposals from those who suggest them. "On the theoretical level," one could say, "I completely agree with you. In the real world, we have to be more pragmatic." Good idealism cannot argue with pragmatism, because if ideals cannot materialize, then they are absolutely useless, especially when the goal of every liberal is to be freer. Why claim greater freedom if it cannot take shape?

Blue sky thinking is useless if you don't step out of your comfort zone and put theory into practice.

– *Un Modelo Realmente Liberal,*
Juan Ramón Rallo

PESSIMIST OR OPTIMIST

Here's a five-second guide to being a genius: Walk into any meeting without preparing, look as if you are listening intently and then pronounce, with a deep sigh: "I can see some problems with this." It doesn't matter what was being discussed, people will assume that you have been blessed with the gift of prophecy and that you are thinking several steps ahead. The guide on how to come across as a fool is equally concise: Just say "what a brilliant idea!" to whatever is proposed. People will assume you are one of those happy-go-lucky simpletons whose very presence jeopardizes everything.

Favouring pessimism is hard-wired into us for the simple reason that the genes for worrying had a greater chance of survival, as they made carriers more cautious. Fortunately, most of us don't risk being killed, eaten or slain on a daily basis anymore but the genetic programme labelled 'worry!' is still encoded in us. This is why pessimistic chief economists are viewed as wise and utopian entrepreneurs considered naïve. Above all, each side will view the other with disdain and simply describe themselves as realists while pointing to supporting historical examples.

Alas, neither side is right.

– *The Future Book,*
Magnus Lindkvist

Pessimism and optimism are lenses through which we transform reality into a kind of moral fable.

BOILING FROGS

Many organizations today are like frogs swimming in slowly heated water. Unaware of the forthcoming danger, they are complacent. They are unwilling to change, shift to a better place, and jump out of the increasingly dangerous hot water and move to safety.

Traditionally managed organizations resemble super-tankers that struggle to respond to sudden changes in their environment and fail to change course in time. Modern organizations should be managed and led like sailboats – a general direction is to be determined, but the journey towards the destination should be flexible, depending on the environmental conditions.

Emergent leadership is based on people, purpose, collaboration, trust, transparency, community and autonomy. Authority is distributed and decisions are based on knowledge rather than on a formal position in organizational hierarchies. Organizations are managed holistically as complex adaptive systems. The new approach brings better engagement, productivity, innovation and profit – this is the future of work and we can implement it now.

Only by a complete change in leadership mindset can we rescue the frogs from the warming water and set them free.

Organizations are being killed slowly by their own inertia.

– Vlatka Hlupic for *Dialogue*

PARALYSIS BY ANALYSIS

We live in an age of information overload. For those who care to seek it out, we have more information than we could possibly process coherently. A phrase has even been coined, summing up this scenario: paralysis by analysis. So if there was ever a time to communicate only the relevant information, it would be now.

The issue is in determining just what is relevant and to whom is it relevant. The issue increases in complexity with project teams and the communication between team members. Adding to this complexity is the communications from team leaders upwards to sponsors and back downwards to team members.

Since it is quite difficult and time-consuming for team leaders and team members to sort through all of the incoming information and feedback from the project, different model utilizations are required.

Relevant communication allows for all information to be communicated so that nothing is missed.

– *Plus Change,*
Moe Glenner

MATCH THE CLIENT

The idea of matching, mirroring or level-selling when choosing your team is a principle of rapport-building – we tend to like and follow people who we think are like us. The challenge is to match your team members with their opposite numbers in the client in terms of role, grade and experience. Common sense suggests that the people who will be working closest together on the contract need to get on and see eye to eye both professionally and personally.

We must also match the client's diversity in terms of age, race and gender, especially in the voluntary and community sector. I heard about a company bidding for a contract to audit a regional drug rehabilitation charity. The bidder sent along three white, middle-aged males… only to find that the selection panel comprised two Afro-Caribbean women and a young white male. The mismatch was stark.

Mirroring the client is also about recognizing their psychological needs, such as needing 'comfort'. This is typically provided by fielding a senior person in your team, often referred to as 'the grey hair' or the 'safe pair of hands'. Their 'been there, done that, got the T-shirt' experience reassures the client that the team is unlikely to be thrown by an issue or obstacle they've never seen before.

Use this reassurance factor in bids where you're facing a new bidder on the block.

– *Winner Takes All*,
Scott Keyser

THE CSR

The brands that listen and respond to their stakeholders' expectations and demands are responsible brands, those championing corporate social responsibility. These brands not only develop social action programs but also build strategies that generate values for the company and for society. Corporate social responsibility begins as a simple philanthropy before turning into social action. From the protection and prevention of risks, it has become a spring-board for differentiation, competitive advantage, growth and the creation of values.

The return of corporate social responsibility has three pillars:

- The recruitment and retention of talent: with a diversification that attracts new employees more efficiently and commits to current employees.
- Social business opportunities: with a diversification based on innovation (in new products and services, in new business models and in new segments of the population).
- Eligibility: a diversification that attracts shareholders and investors.

Clear communication with both employees and customers is vital to business success.

– Atrapados por el Consumo,
Xavier Oliver & Ángel Alloza

EIGHT GOLDEN RULES

1. Set a vision for your brand, then define it and make it relevant in the market.
2. Remember the heritage of your brand and maintain a direct reference to your story.
3. Have tight control of your distribution and try to avoid unofficial 'grey market' imports.
4. Make sure the quality of your materials is exceptional
5. The design of luxury brand goods has to be perfect – as if we need reminding.
6. The 'hand of man' should still be evident and craftsmanship has to be exquisite – from the stitching to the finish.
7. Stick to the brand code and make sure you use a 'brand language'. If you keep an obsession with the level of detail in your language, this means it will become more recognizable.
8. Service – the human factor – is a huge part of being a luxury brand. This describes the everyday 'mythology' of the brand, and how well the people stick to the brand code and implement it in their deals with customers on a daily basis.

**What is luxury?
Something we
don't need.
But what is a
luxury brand?**

– James Ogilvy for *Dialogue*

TRANSLATING KNOWLEDGE

Knowledge as a resource always relates to people. But people are not an asset in the legal sense – organizations cannot own people, as suppliers and the service are indivisible. People, per se, are motivated. Self-responsibility is the dominant source of motivation. Purpose is a necessary condition for motivation. Moreover, people have the ability to reflect (pre-frontal cortex as the executive function of humans to initiate, engage and decide) and re-act (sensory cortex) as the reflexive mode of operation. As Peter Drucker (1967) concludes: "In times when knowledge is the critical resource, all people are executives, accept the fact that we have to treat almost anybody as a volunteer."

To cope with the challenges of a turbulent era (the 'outer game') and simultaneously benefit from the knowledge of the talent (the 'inner game'), we need to build a bridge between the talent and organizations that cater to people. Management needs a design that enables that bridge to a superior ability to act. Some say management has only one client: the employee.

– Management Design,
Lukas Michel

Knowledge that is not used is of no value to an organization.

BRAND MANAGEMENT

Some of the rules for good brand management are timeless truths:

- Protect your brand: the name of your brand and company, your logo and colours, the shape of your packaging, the scents and even the sounds in your advertisements.
- Pursue the satisfaction of all stakeholders: your customers expect attractive products and services that meet their expectations. Your employees want to work for a company with an attractive business idea to which they feel committed. Your shareholders expect solid management of the company and a commitment to increase the value they receive. Your business partners want to negotiate with fairness and respect and see how the company's reputation adds value to yours.
- Treat your brand as an investment, not as a cost. Brands are among the most important assets that a business owns and the strongest can guarantee the continuity of the company in challenging times.
- Exploit the financial potential of your brand through the development of new products and techniques, such as sharing brands, licensing and creating franchises.
- Understand that managing a brand successfully requires skills that go beyond traditional marketing functions.

Successfully managing brands enables them to be a strategic asset of the company.

– *En Clave de Marcas,*
Gonzalo Brujó

GETTING EMOTIONAL

One of the biggest challenges you will face as an entrepreneur is when the time comes to decide whether to sell the business you founded, let someone else run it or continue to stay in control. At the beginning, as an entrepreneur you are convinced that it is only you who can lead your start-up to huge success. When you start off as an entrepreneur, your business idea is normally just that – an idea only. You are the person who has the belief, desire and vision to build a great business from your initial idea. It is you who can see the opportunity that your innovative product or service will provide and you are determined to capitalize on it. So, you go for it and secure the finance you need to start the business. If it looks like things are going well, then you hire the people to help build the business according to your vision and you develop close relationships with those first employees. You might take on the role of the CEO, but not always. Whatever your role is, you create the culture of the business, which normally is an extension of your personality, and you set the agenda. From the start, employees, customers and suppliers identify your business with you, the founder. You then start to have some success and your business grows.

New ventures are usually labours of love for entrepreneurs and they become emotionally attached to them.

– *The Entrepreneur's Book,*
Neil Francis

DELIBERATE DAYDREAMING

In the 1950s, psychology researcher Jerome Singer found that slipping into a daydream was not helpful, nor was it helpful to guiltily ruminate over things. Yet, there is one type of daydreaming that will help you to become more creative and even re-energize your brain: Positive Constructive Daydreaming (PCD).

PCD must be built into your day, deliberately.

After withdrawing your attention from the outside, use playful and wishful imagery. For some, this might be lying on a yacht. For others, it may involve running through the woods. Whatever the image, do this while doing something low-key, like knitting or gardening. Doing nothing at all is not as effective.

With PCD, your brain switches to 'default' mode and, when it does, your unconscious can work its magic by stimulating innovative ideas and even helping you predict the future more effectively.

Identify times of the day when your energy is low, such as mid-morning, after lunch, mid-afternoon and at the end of your day. Build in a 10-15-minute period of PCD.

It may seem like you are wasting time, but you should think of it as refuelling your brain.

Embrace distraction – don't avoid it.

– Srini Pillay for *Dialogue*

HIDDEN AGENDAS

Think about this. Every day all over the world people enter the workplace with their own personal preoccupations: work pressures, health concerns, money worries, family problems, relationship issues, political viewpoints and more. That's a lot of variables to consider. And these are the easy ones because they're the things that people are generally aware of – conscious of – although they can still impact their work and be difficult for others to cope with.

But the ones that they haven't got a clue about – the ones that are unconscious – are the really tricky ones like unresolved childhood and family issues, fears, anxieties, fantasies, drives, prejudices, obsessions, and complicated emotions like anger and guilt. That's what is happening when you sabotage something you've been striving for, such as a promotion or a deal – or when someone gets angry with you for no obvious reason. You become upset and confused because the behavior is illogical. And that is indeed the problem.

– The Conscious Leader,
Shelley Reciniello

Unconscious cultures begin at the top.

CHANGING GENERATIONS

Most of today's consumer packaged goods (CPG) marketers are in the business of creating superior-performing products that meet unmet consumer needs. Their orientation is need centric and their consumer learning process is built to seek out problems or issues that current products don't address. They seek out problems so as to design solutions, which has led to a popular format of advertising used for decades: problem/ solution.

The Boomers grew up with these kinds of ads. Who could forget classics like, "Hate that gray/Wash it away with Clairol," or "Those dirty rings around the collar/ Wisk around the collar beats ring around the collar" or "Dishpan hands/ Use Palmolive"?

In marketing to the aging consumer, the problem with the problem/solution approach is the problem itself. Aging Boomers don't see themselves as having problems. Yes, unexpected things do happen as part of aging, but it's much more pleasant to rationalize them as changes, i.e., normal things that happen as one's body changes. As a generation that was born during a time of unprecedented optimism, it's only natural for them to avoid the negativity of problems in preference for a positive outlook on age-related developments.

There is scientific evidence that people get happier as they get older.

– *The Old Rush,*
Peter Hubbell

CORPORATE ENTREPRENEURSHIP

Corporate entrepreneurship offers, along with many other benefits, a timely means to promote your own project without having to bet the house and throw yourself into an uncertain entrepreneurial adventure, which can more often than not result in failure. Thanks to the support of an appropriate corporate environment, uncertainty becomes a medium risk bet, a leap with a network of proper courses of action.

The practice of corporate entrepreneurship must be progressively introduced into the company's day-to-day business via adaptive tools and programs, which must evolve in line with the maturity of each organization, the development of its capabilities and the requirements of the environment. It is not a fad, but a key feature for the survival of the company in a global and highly competitive environment, where the search for disruptive innovations is a fundamental pillar for growth. The world moves at a great speed. Technology evolves rapidly. Globalization increases competitiveness and weakens barriers to entry. Economic power is shifting towards Asia and the emerging countries. Companies must take their innovative procedures and corporate entrepreneurship very seriously if they do not want to compromise their viability.

– *Impulso,*
Joan Riera & Tomás Soler

> **Corporate entrepreneurship is a vital feature in any innovation plan that does not proceed from chance or luck but by allowing people to fail.**

MEASURE OF SUCCESS

Would it make sense to invent other measures of success for companies and industries? Is the viability criterion applicable to entire countries, or does the absence of such a measure mean that there is an undisclosed desire to circumvent delicately the fact that sooner or later all systems will see the same fate? I think that this is the reason why the term 'competitiveness' is used more often than 'viability' in the economic domain. In each cycle of innovation, at each new loop of evolution, the same functions are put into action in order to make the four-leaf clover blossom – creation, integration, competition and filtration (selection). This results in accumulation of social wealth, represented by one of the leaves of the lucky clover, the leaf that makes it possible to create a reserve of 'energy' for the next phase of adaptation.

The process itself is interesting and captivating, as it requires people at each loop to create something completely new – something that will define that wealth itself will take. In advance of further narrative, I will say that the process is not linear and takes place with a time lag. Sometimes an innovation is implemented decades after the invention was made. Innovations penetrate into other areas step by step, gradually accumulating a certain critical mass.

It is those who manage to 'commercialize innovation' before others that reap the lion's share of the profit.

– *Humanity's Lucky Clover,*
Vadim Makhov

PHILOSOPHICAL TECHNOLOGY

The fashion business has long grappled with the problems of environmental protection in the face of massive consumption of material resources. Numerous projects and initiatives have been suggested and pursued, but to limited effect. For ecological concepts to truly take a central place in this industry, and across our society as a whole, we clearly must adopt a new all-round, multi-level scientific philosophy. A good model, or at least a starting point, might be the ancient Greeks' philosophical approach to science and the natural world. The Greeks realized that it was possible to recognize patterns and predictable recurrences and relationships, hidden in nature. And those patterns, they came to understand, held the key to unlocking the secrets of the world around us.

One could argue that a country's vitality can be measured exclusively through Gross National Product (GNP), the market value of all products and services produced in a year. But beyond the churning wheels of heavy industry, it's my heartfelt belief that an unlikely field like the fashion business can indeed lead to a better way of life. In fact, there's growing recognition that the advancement of fashion, and its intersection with art and culture, is good for a community's overall sense of economic health and wellbeing.

– *Wholegarment,*
Shuhei Aida

Focus on the nuts and bolts of engineering evolved into a combination of science and art to become 'technology'.

BE COMPETITIVE

There are two deeply ingrained beliefs regarding our workday: that being at work is the same as working, and that leaving last, or doing it after the boss has gone, is cause for celebration and distinction. Both are wrong, not to say unsuitable for the 21st century. Only the minutes we take advantage of in the service of our responsibilities to the company are productive, not those we spend merely keeping our chairs warm. However, this message is still not assimilated enough, neither among managers nor among employees. Thus, Spain is one of the most unproductive countries in Europe, despite being one of those dedicating the most hours to work. Maybe it is precisely because of this emphasis on hours that Spain remains this way. We know that productivity decreases after a certain number of hours. It's normal. People are not robots or machines.

It is about working with objectives and results, and not about rewarding being present. This does not guarantee good productivity. The paradoxical culture of presenteeism must be substituted with a culture of efficiency, and even of excellence. Only then can we be competitive in an increasingly complex and globalized world.

Presenteeism doesn't guarantee productivity so avoid rewarding out of hours working and instead encourage a healthy balance from your employees.

– *Dejemos de Perder el Tiempo,*
Jorge Cagigas & Ignacio Buqueras

SOURCE OF WEALTH

In recent years, the academic discipline of wealth research has become well established, and several doctoral dissertations and collections of essays have been published on this topic. One gap in the research relates to the group that will be referred to in this book as the 'wealth elite' or 'ultra-high-net-worth individuals' (UHNWIs). These are individuals who have accumulated net assets in the tens or hundreds of millions. There are hardly any findings that relate to the creation of wealth within this group, or to the personality traits and behavioural patterns that have enabled their economic success.

Additionally, academic wealth researchers have so far failed to give due consideration to the findings of another research field, namely entrepreneurship research. This comes as something of a surprise, as the results of entrepreneurship research are also of great interest to academic wealth researchers, because a substantial majority of wealthy people became wealthy as entrepreneurs. In particular, academic wealth researchers have so far failed to fully exploit the broad spectrum of research on the correlation between specific personality traits and entrepreneurial success.

The most important prerequisite for accumulating substantial wealth from paid work is self-employment.

– *The Wealth Elite,*
Rainer Zitelmann

AUTHENTIC BEHAVIOUR

The key context for organizations is that the pace of change has never been faster and continues to accelerate. This situation is fuelled by our ability to communicate information at lightning speed to millions of people. We have a voracious appetite for new knowledge and live in a world of unprecedented complexity. Collaboration and outsourcing has created more and more virtual organizations.

But against this dynamic landscape blurred by speed and change, we remain, at our core, human beings with some basic and simple characteristics. We are emotional beings in need of a sense of purpose and a sense of belonging. These base needs are very powerful. The traditional role of the organization was to bring order, direction and control. But as the world becomes more dynamic, this approach is less and less relevant. It is more appropriate to have flexibility of objectives, action and reaction; to be able to adapt, to be agile. It takes too long for the traditional command and control approach to respond. Decentralized decision making is needed but within a constancy of 'way' or core personality.

Organizations are judged on the behaviour of the people representing them.

– *The 31 Practices,*
Alan Williams &
Dr Alison Whybrow

CENTRE LEADERS

Centre-Leaders play a critical boundary-spanning role in ensuring the leadership system effectively balances and iterates around a top-down directive approach and bottom-up participatory approach to formulating and executing strategy.

They also proactively navigate the 'Change/People polarity', ensuring innovation is nurtured and that people are fully engaged and motivated to adopt the next practices, routines and behaviours required to ensure organization survival and encourage ongoing renewal. Centre-Leaders function as shock absorbers within the organization by anticipating constant disequilibrium, potential distresses and working from the middle-out to ensure that the organization has the requisite resilience to absorb the shock.

We must recognize that the design of a VUCA-ready leadership system begins by cultivating collective catalytic action within a group of Centre-Leaders who share a common aspiration to take both their organizations and their people to the next level.

Winning leaders of the future distribute power from the centre. They no longer sit at the top.

– Tony O'Driscoll for *Dialogue*

RISE AND FALL

Pax Japonica will soon come true, because the global community will urgently need enormous allowance for bad debts. It'll be the secret assets held by Japan's Imperial House that will make tremendous contributions to this issue, which will be endorsed by the Western leadership and simultaneously backed by the traditional leadership of the whole Chinese nation.

Facing the accelerating irregularity of solar activities, the Western leadership is trying to get rid of the current situation by boosting technological innovation with negative real interest rates. Nevertheless, this historical attempt is doomed to fail, since the majority of humankind still tends to stick to conventional manners and structures. As no technological innovations will ever give us any kind of fundamental breakthrough, the global economy will be hyper inflated due to previous overwhelming quantitative easing in various countries. Of course, Japan, as a state with enormous sovereign debt, will fall into severe crisis before anything else.

Something much more decisive is needed to push forward human civilization.

– Pax Japonica,
Takeo Harada

VISIONARY LEADERSHIP

Before inspiring others, the leader must be first inspired. Defining spirituality in the context of leadership is a good gauge for inspiration. Inspiration is personal and specific to each leader, and where it occurs varies from one person to the next. Though some find inspiration within themselves, others find it in the outside world, and many in both realms, all being both inspired and having the ability to inspire others.

The most notable characteristic of visionary and effective leaders is their firm insistence on defending their personal values. Visionary leadership is based on a balanced expression of the spiritual, mental, emotional and physical dimensions, and requires basic values, a clear vision, supportive relationships and innovative actions. When one or more dimensions are missing, leadership will fail at manifesting such a vision.

All visionary leaders, who embody a sense of personal integrity and radiate energy, vitality and will, possess the outstanding characteristic to show a commitment to values. The will is to remain in a spiritual state of being. It is a spiritual attribute allowing the leader to represent something.

What visionary values does your company have?

– Coaching por Valores,
Simon Dolan

FABRIC OF TRUST

Trust is one of the most talked about themes within organizations. Many people express their desire for a higher level of trust, and hope that teambuilding sessions and leadership development programmes will help nurture that trust. Retreats, coaching and professional development courses can help, but they aren't a magic bullet. Why is this the case? Because deeper layers of anxiety just don't get addressed and staying too polite in the safe (easy) zone does nothing to build trust.

One of the key roles of senior leaders is to reduce anxiety and create an environment of trust, where people can deliver their best. Trust is a result – an outcome from an ongoing process. To build and reinforce the fabric of trust requires a systematic process. It starts with understanding the dynamics of anxieties within the team and learning how to shift them, both across the group and at a personal level. Anything that does not address this in depth will not work in the long run.

The more we reveal about ourselves, the more others will get to know us in different ways, the more reliable we will become.

– Leading From Behind,
Dirk Devos, Manon De Wit
& Robert Lubberding

LIVING WITH DIGNITY

One of the greatest virtues is human dignity and Western culture has gradually discovered its importance. It is what makes us live as we are. It is our intrinsic quality. Dignity must govern our conscience, our life.

Our future will depend on dignity. Without it, nobody can be happy. Nobody. Because it has the quality of increasing our degree of consciousness, self-esteem and respect. However, we must take into account that a very thin line exists between dignity and ego. We have to be very careful not to overdo it and, therefore, hurt interpersonal relationships.

In the same way, we should be aware that the only way people lose their dignity is when they give up on it. They can tear off your arms and legs against your will. They can drag your body across the floor, but they can never trample your dignity if you don't allow it. So it's you who decides whether your dignity remains intact or for sale, bargained, trampled or at the mercy of another.

– Del Vientre a la Muerte,
Chandra Choubey

How can you maintain your dignity in a society that has lost essential values?

GENERATE KINDNESS

In the business world, kindness and generosity are essential for happiness. They also contribute to improving performance. Kindness, or the absence of it, propagates within collective emotions and is a fundamental trait of each organization's culture. Kindness is not only good for those who receive it but also, and especially, for those who practise it. One way to manage our levels of kindness is to keep a diary of kind actions: I helped a partner to finish a job; swapped my vacation with a person in need; invited a newcomer to eat out; changed my shift with another employee, etc. Keeping a diary of kindness helps us to remember the moment when we took the opportunity to be kind, which in turn generated positive emotions and also new healthy emotions.

Expressing gratitude can be considered a meta-strategy for achieving happiness: grateful people have more energy and are more optimistic. They experience positive emotions more often, tend to be kinder and are more sympathetic, spiritual and forgiving than those who are less predisposed to gratitude.

Encouraging kindness, generosity and gratitude in your company will not only improve people's happiness but their productivity.

– *La Felicidad en el Trabajo y en la Vida*, Santiago Vázquez

MENTAL WELLBEING

Anyone can suffer a period of mental ill health. It can emerge very suddenly, develop as the result of a specific event or rear its head gradually and worsen over time. Some mental health conditions can be persistent and may be classed as a 'disability' while others might come and go, giving you 'good' days and 'bad' days. And, although some of us might be diagnosed with a mental health condition, with the right support we can still enjoy a healthy, productive and happy life.

Regardless of where you are on the mental health spectrum, it is important to remember that, if you have a problem, with the right support and treatment you can and will get better. In fact, you will often recover completely. When we have positive mental health we can, as individuals, realize our full potential, cope with the stress and challenges that day-to-day life throws at us, work productively, and be a meaningful and contributing member of our communities.

Your mental health, just like your physical health, is impacted by a range of factors, environments and experiences. Some of these might be out of your control, whereas others can be influenced by you and those around you.

Our mental health is also a key factor in the decisions and choices we make in our lives.

– Positive Male Mind,
Dr Shaun Davis & Andrew Kinder

FOUNDATIONS OF OUR EMOTIONS

Living brands incorporate the very forces of human life. They're based on the fundamentals of our biology and neurobiology and the rich hierarchy of inherent concepts they infuse into our everyday life.

Marketing and consumer research today are largely based on psychology. However, the roots of human behaviour lie in biology, not in psychology. In establishing the links between many disciplines, Living Brands follows the neurobiological origins of concepts and the tracks our brain uses to create them and puts forward the most integrated tool to date for understanding brands, categories and consumer behaviour. It can help marketers generate seminal ideas for brand positioning, communication and creative development that activate the inherent concepts in our brain, impacting the way emotions and habits are formed.

The causes of our behavior are rooted in human dispositions that have helped us survive and thrive. To ensure that we never forget the importance of these life-affirming forces, nature has established an array of systems in our brain and body and made their satisfaction intrinsically gratifying.

As abundant and varied as our emotions are, they all stem from 12 Fundamental Human Motives.

– *Living Brands,*
Constantinos Pantidos

BENEVOLENT DICTATORS

Indians have embraced old British customs of hierarchy and there is high degree of formality between colleagues. It is common to call a superior 'sir' or 'madam'. Similarly, influences of Hinduism and caste have created a culture that emphasizes established hierarchical relationships. All relationships therefore observe hierarchy. The idea of hierarchy is deeply rooted in the Indian psyche. Hierarchical relationships are important in the business context.

Working 'through proper channels' is highly emphasized. For example, if you are looking for a quick result on some licence application, take time to study the hierarchical set up of the office to which you've submitted it. If you respect the office hierarchy, your work gets done faster. Students call teachers 'guru' and at work 'the boss' is considered the ultimate source of responsibility and power. Hierarchical relationships mean bosses tell subordinates what to do and how to do it, and seeking permission from those above is a sign of respect. In India, bosses are like benevolent dictators who look out for their teams.

Make it clear from the outset if you want independently-minded employees.

– Nikhil Raval for *Dialogue*

VALUE PROPOSITION

A company's value proposition describes the benefits customers expect to get from the products and services provided by the company. It is often composed of one or more statements that succinctly explain the causality between the customer needs that the company strives to satisfy and its own survival and development. The most fundamental aspects of a value proposition have been and will always be high quality, good services, reasonable prices and fast response to changes in customer needs. This is all that customers want and that will never change. At the same time, the value proposition must target customers' pain points. Only when a company considers all these factors in its value proposition can the value proposition truly attract customers' attention and guide the company's business operations.

The value proposition of a company stems from the value propositions of its customers. It is the driving force that helps set the company apart from the competition, the company's starting point and ultimate goal when it designs its competition strategies, and the core of the company's business model. A business model is, in essence, the way a company delivers its value proposition and receives financial returns in the process.

Our core values are the key to our success.

– *Customer Centricity,*
Huang Weiwei

BANK REFERENCE

Although finance is considered a purely global activity, commercial banking does not lend itself to international expansion. The reason lies in the multi-economic, regulatory, political and cultural barriers fragmenting markets from country to country. Perhaps this characteristic calls for the publishing of a book about one of the few banks that has managed to overcome these obstacles.

It is precisely what the Bank of Santander has managed over a very short period, starting from a country of origin usually not considered as an incubator for large financial institutions. The Bank of Santander demonstrates that, in the global economy, structural disadvantages can be overcome in a creative way. Its rapid rise, as one of the ten largest banks in the world, shows that the best way to become a leader within a certain context of an otherwise accelerating and changing world is to act decisively and to take calculated risks.

It is the only major bank in the world in which four successive generations of the same family have exercised an important influence over its top executives and board of directors.

– Santander, el Banco,
Mauro Guillén

Exercising business expertise alongside calculated risks is key to providing a rival service to your competitors.

AN INIMITABLE PuRODUCT

What led to the transformation of silk from a Chinese fiber to an icon of luxury through the ages? To answer this question, we must first understand the product and meet the traders and markets involved in the globalization of silk. We must assess their contributions in the context of their own cultural, economic and political environment.

Our research brings us from Antiquity through the post Roman age all the way to modern times. This is a story that began about 5,000 years ago and perhaps even longer. It spanned the rise and fall of great empires: Greece's Hellenistic Age, Parthian, Bactrian, Roman, Persian, Chinese, Kushan, Byzantine, Islam, Mongol, Ottoman Turks and the Europeans. Its geography spans from the Far East to the West. Along with the rise in trade, silk embraced the beginning, development and propagation of three world religions: Buddhism, Christianity and

The silk textile spurred the development of other industrial applications expanding its reach and utility across vast global markets.

Islam. Sitting at all crossroads, silk witnessed the birth and rebirth of connections between the East and the West and multitudes of defining wars and conflicts. Each ending was simply a new beginning.

– *Silk Through the Ages,*
Trini Callava

TRIANGLES AND PYRAMIDS

The triangle is a design classic.

It captures the essence of any 1, 2, 3 or A, B, C sequence so beloved of people the world over.

Three blind mice. An Englishman, an Irishman and a Scotsman walk into a bar. The Lord of the Rings trilogy. Everybody loves things that come in threes.

So, if any three-pronged issue requires explanation, try a triangle. But there's more.

Wedges can dramatize gradual increases or declines – building a story up, or narrowing options down.

Interlocking two triangles can show a mixture of both, or a transition from one state of affairs to another.

Pyramids can explain gradation and the components of a progression.

And, rather brilliantly, the space in the middle of a triangle offers a chance for a fourth component – most powerfully, the focal point of the issue in question.

– *The Diagrams Book,*
Kevin Duncan

Diagrams are superb for organising your own thinking.

THE SAFE BUSINESS

A good franchise project relies on strong piloting. It should implicitly consider a start-up and follow-up period that actually allow for the verification of whether results meet expectations, whether the business model functions as anticipated, the composition of its commercial offer, and the operating procedures for administration, management, marketing policies and facilities.

Only with a careful and well-programmed follow-up of the pilot units can we collect the actual management data and obtain operating ratios with which we can adjust the provisional financial plans.

Piloting a franchise implies perfecting the two building blocks of the system it represents. On one hand, the business goals for the franchised activity, and, on the other, the organization that supports the associative relationship defined by the franchise agreement. For this reason, it is advisable to do the piloting not only with official units but also with the collaboration and contributions of a small list of franchisees; the chain's first disciples, those who take part in it with this clear objective, and who can harvest a concrete income, that is defined and valued in advance.

Conducting pilot schemes ensures the validity and sustainability of a franchise project.

– *50 Claves Para Franquiciar,*
Mariano Alonso

YOUR BODY, YOUR HEALTH

If you suffer from poor health, get it fixed. Don't suffer. Of course, there are times when that warrants a trip to the doctor's surgery and this is certainly the place to go if you have any serious worries about your health. The problem comes when the only solution is a pill for every ailment and there appears to be no real solution to your problem except another pill to stop the side effect of the last one. Poor health isn't caused by a deficiency in prescriptions.

Niggly health problems – like digestive troubles, minor stress issues, mild depression or anxiety, and feeling tired – can only really be solved by you. First steps: blood sugar control, avoid twaddle food, go for real food and cut the sugar. If your health is compromised, it's time to focus on the details until it's fixed.

- If the problem is serious (or you are worried), go to the doctor.
- If they send you away without a real solution, take matters into your own hands. Get to the root cause of the issue. Address your diet and how you are living your life.
- Making a change is going to take a bit of effort – exercise, relaxation, food and sleep.

Remember there might be a lot you can contribute to your own health by taking action.

– *Positive Nutrition,*
Kate Cook

TECH IS NOT INNOVATION

Think about the hammer. If you can't hit straight, or don't know which end to use, no matter how great your hammer is, it's not going to knock in a nail. It's only of any use to you if you know what to do with it. It's the same with tech. One of the consequences of digital is that people see it as an end, rather than a tool.

Sure, we can work faster on a Mac Pro than with pen and ink. We have many more channels to engage customers through technology. We can adapt and change our ideas more quickly than before. We can share projects instantly.

But some have become so bogged down in the momentary joy of the latest device that they forget that some of the best campaigns in the world began with a pencil and a great idea.

The tech 'geeks' need to sit down with the creative 'freaks' and collaborate. Use the tools of technology in innovative ways. Just pushing your campaign out through every device under the sun isn't innovation, it's distribution.

Some of the best ideas in the world start with a pencil and a well-trained ear.

– Tracy Wong for *Dialogue*

OPENING BOUNDARIES

Ten years ago, Huawei's finance staff were criticized non-stop. They were criticized by our CEO Mr Ren Zhengfei, by business departments, by customers and by employees. We were like a headless chicken, running around aimlessly and constantly weighed down by our work.

Today, 10 years later, we are still criticized. But the criticism is different now. Criticisms of finance are no longer about blame or complaining. The criticisms we receive these days express expectation, tolerance, patience, drive and encouragement. We are like a tiny sapling yearning to grow. We are working hard and constantly improving.

In the past, we would improve only after we were aware of our weaknesses. We would take up our responsibilities and stumble our way forward into the light. Today, we have a plan and act accordingly. We remain dedicated to our beliefs and work hard to create value.

Only by properly managing every project can an enterprise maintain robust operations.

– Visionaries: Huawei Stories,
Tian Tao & Yin Zhifeng

PARADIGM SHIFT

The requirements for both management and organizations have evolved continuously during the last century, correlating with advancements in psychology, the arts, music, technology, the political landscape and society.

It's hard to put a finger on a specific time or event marking the change, but the driver and the cause of the development is often said to be technological advancement. The propagation of the internet and computers is one of the clearest vital signs of the change, since it has made global communication and access to knowledge easy. We are always 'online'. Crowd-sourcing, artificial intelligence (AI), and automation are possible, both with robots and software. This has dramatically influenced the customer's behaviour and attitude to the market, the employee's relationship to organizations and work, and management and leaders' roles and behaviours. It has also played a role in connecting the world and enabling globalisation – supporting or even advancing societal development.

We are looking into a future with constant change.

– *The Responsive Leader,*
Erik Korsvik Østergaard

CAPTAIN MADE OF WOOD

Balance, intuition, perception ... what are the elements to keep a team of football players strong and united? When does the winning spirit peak? What about ambition? Does it have a limit? Can we truly lose the hunger to win?

The part that captains play (managers, along with coaches in charge of leading sports projects), are that of beacons. They help light the path of young footballers, newly signed recruits, the many clueless foreigners who do not understand the idiosyncrasies of the club they have just joined, the homegrown players who believe they can spend the rest of their lives in an afternoon of glory, and all those who respect the traditional values of football as experienced in a locker room.

Leaders do not last very long without the support of others. You can think of yourself a leader, have a high opinion of yourself, but it is the others, your collaborators, who grant you the title. They say that from Monday to Friday players should be treated like people, and on Sundays like footballers. It is a strategy, one of many of course, to keep the staff alert and in harmony.

Being part of a team means working together and supporting each other for success.

– Capitanes,
Luis Villarejo

LIBERAL IDEOLOGY

Everyone knows that liberalism has two major problems to face and solve. Put in a nutshell, the first says that the two other ideologies – conservatism and socialism – in all their degrees, are immersed in a necessary renewal and updating process. They still do not know how to do it or what to do. For this reason, they have decided to save as much time as possible by clinging to what suits them in liberalism and to the most extreme pragmatism and opportunism, even when this stance contradicts their traditional ideological essence. Defining oneself as 'conservative liberal' or social-ist 'according to liberals' sounds positive and elegant, but there is a lot of contradiction in the terms. In the end, con-servatives conserve and socialists socialize.

The second problem of liberalism lies in the difficult precision of its ideology, partly because of the manipulation that has already been mentioned and partly because liber-als have devoted little effort to specifying it and making it accessible. It is not an impossible task. It only has to start by affirm-ing that liberals, logically, defend all freedoms, big and small.

Does he who limits his liber-alism to defend the market economy take this ideology to an unacceptable reductionism?

– *Ideas en Libertad*,
Garrigues Walker

DESIGN MATTERS

Simplicity is difficult to achieve; it requires hard work. Apple had set a benchmark in the mobile phone market, creating intuitive products that are pleasurable to use. I wanted to use Apple and the iPhone as the inspiration for the look and feel and usage of Heartbeat. In a relatively short time – think back to the mobile phones at the beginning of this century – Apple became a leader in transforming the way we communicate. This tiny device we hold in our hands now contains much of the essential data for conducting our lives, but particularly for conveying instant information about the emotions we are feeling at any given moment. Why has all this happened so quickly and, it seems, across the whole human race, in all countries and cultures, among people of every kind? Much of it has to do with design.

The technology and the software are crucial, but we should not underestimate the effect of Apple's graphics. This is design that starts from a deep analysis and understanding of how human beings might use the product.

If other mobile phone companies could learn from Apple, why couldn't we?

– Revolution in a Heartbeat,
Matt Stephens

INTERNATIONAL SUCCESS

Design and trading is the soul of Zara, even if this is not where the creative process begins or ends. On the physical level, Zara is about huge open spaces. It does away with cubicles, rooms or offices, which would emphasize devotion or responsibility. Large but light, the desks are grouped by product specialties: women, men, young people, infants, sports, and combine the commercial and design world without a sense of continuity. Nothing differentiates the executive from the newcomer, except by observing who has received the most enquiries in the different zones. These latter are only identifiable by noticing what dominant type of objects are scattered around the desks: photos, patterns, shreds of garments, drawings, magazine clippings – an apparently chaotic assortment of inspiration and creativity around computers, which designers use to create, adjust and transpose the data that commercial partners provide. Creative chaos? Maybe.

Embrace open spaces and open communication if you want to nature innovation and creativity.

Clothes are everywhere: on tables, racks and chairs ... but hardly anything around the mannequins, contrary to what anyone would think.

– *Zara y sus Hermanos*,
Enrique Badía

DOUBLE TASKING

It's a sure sign you've reached the land of the two 'O's (overwhelmed and overcommitted) when your productivity engine has you attempting two or more things at a time. Busy days can see you emailing while on a conference call, attending a meeting while mentally preparing for the next one, working on two documents, messaging and mentally planning your evening, all at the same time.

Brain science has shown that you can only truly be effective at one conscious task (and that goes for men and women!). As soon as you mentally split on more than one, while it appears possible, you will block access to subconscious capabilities that could liberate your full potential.

Below your conscious surface you are busy sensing things: the environment you are in, the sounds, sights, feelings, smells and tastes all around you. These brilliant sensory clues sharpen your ability to know what's going on at a given moment. In addition to this, your amazing brain will be accessing files and information to match the sensory data. And, all the while, you will be tuning into your intuitive creative subconscious.

> **You don't get double-brilliance by double-tasking, more likely half-and-half.**

– The "Keep It Simple" Book,
Simon Tyler

TRUSTING TOO EASY

For one week in 2012, social psychologist Dr Adam DI Kramer launched an experiment using the world's biggest laboratory of human behaviour – Facebook. He wanted to discover the propensity for 'emotional contagion' – do the emotions expressed by our Facebook friends affect our own mood? Tweaking the algorithms to include more positive or negative content, Kramer was able to assess the extent to which posts made users more or less happy.

The experiment became notorious; users complained of being 'lab rats'. Yet, even according to Facebook itself, the chances of users of the platform being experimented upon are precisely 100%. "At any given time," says Dan Farrell, a Facebook data scientist, "any given user will be part of ten experiments the company happens to be conducting." When the University of Illinois surveyed Facebook users, it found that 62% of them were unaware that it manipulated its feed at all. That means that more than 1 billion people think the system instantly and without prejudice shares whatever they or their friends post.

The real truth is out there, but few hear it.

Traffic lights, stop signs, road lanes, airbags and seatbelts arrived decades after the motorcar. Don't trust technology too much, too soon.

– Rachel Botsman for *Dialogue*

PROBABILITY THEORY

Interviewing is a shake of the dice. What we are initiating and utilizing is probability theory; the more opportunities you examine, the higher number of opportunities you will be exposed to. The more decisions you make, the better you get at decision-making. Sure, there will be some bad experiences and some interviews that don't go so well. So what? It will only have the weight you decide to give it.

By reviewing your goals and your *Interview Strategy* notebook daily, you will be able to examine your own strengths and weaknesses which will help you to focus. This will help you to keep your mind away from activities that may disturb your energy.

This brings us to the most critical part of the interview process, the decision-making part. The pressure is undoubtedly immense and can flare up your ulcer, cost you sleep and have you staring at the grass in the back yard as the kids wonder what has gotten into you. This sounds bad and stressful, but it shouldn't be. The fun in choosing your destiny is that you get to reap the benefits of courageous decisions that only you can make.

Anytime we make a decision we create a frame and then use it to see the opportunity, issue and problem.

– *Interview Strategy,*
Jim Finucan

VALUE PEOPLE

How important are people to a company? Let me first tell you a story. In 2006, we acquired a small company that developed a certain kind of processor. We bought the company's source code and all its documentation, but we didn't hire any of the development team. We thought that with the code and the documentation, we could develop products on our own. After two years, however, we had developed nothing. In 2008, we brought the company's core team members on board and very soon they had produced a product. This made us realize that people are the most valuable asset in a company. They are worth much more than source code, designs and documentation.

We also realized that we should properly reward those valuable people. Competition in the future will be our talent against your talent. A company's ability to compete will depend on whether it is able to attract the best people. If we don't offer good opportunities or competitive compensation, we will not attract them.

People are always the most valuable asset.

– Explorers: Huawei Stories,
Tian Tao & Yin Zhifeng

THE JFK BRAND

JFK's presidency lasted 1,032 days, just over three years – a period that served to justify a life, change the style of doing politics and position the United States as a global leader. These thousand days revealed how a new and young generation of politicians, born in the 20th century, could take on the challenges and responsibilities involved in re-launching a nation.

If we ask people today what they remember about JFK, however, almost everyone would confidently reply that it was his way of exercising the presidency, his smile even in times of crisis and difficulties, not only for the United States but also the world, and his unexpected assassination in Dallas.

Live and work in such a way that your life is remembered and inspires future generations.

– JFK,
Salvador Rus

CORPORATE SOCIAL RESPONSIBILITY

The difficult task of getting companies to behave with integrity, to be more aware of the impact of their activities, and the essential aspects that must be addressed within this domain, how such an activity should be implemented and how it actually occurs daily within an organization, can be called social responsibility. It is also described as business ethics, sustainability, social strategy, internal identity and culture, management of relationships with interest groups, or whatever else we wish.

The management of social responsibility had followed a trial-and-error approach for many years. We tried one way and, if it failed, we tried another. Union professionals have, in my opinion, shared the tricks and secrets of transparency and complicity to a very high level. In that world, when a colleague gets ahead, it's everyone's success. Each step that someone takes is shared. It's this consent that makes things possible. I have always said that the best thing social responsibility has given me is people. Though I'm not sure what it is, there's something that all of us in this have in common.

Whatever name you give it, corporate social responsibility can be a complicated task.

– *La Sociedad que No Quería Ser Anónima,* Esther Trujillo

AGE OF ADVERTISING

The global growth and influence of advertising agencies is one of the world's great business success stories. From modest beginnings, the industry has grown and flourished.

Early advertising involved little more than preparing posters or running display ads in newspapers for patent medicines, soaps, cereals and cigarettes. Today, advertising blankets the world via television, movies, magazines, billboards, radio, newspapers, brochures, electronic displays, computer screens, mobile telephones – as well as via T-shirts, coffee mugs, pencils, athletic uniforms and anything else that can either catch the eye or be handed out. Digital and social advertising includes Facebook, Instagram, Snapchat, web pages, games, YouTube videos and tweets that are designed to create involvement with customers (or trade insults with adversaries, as the case may be). An Oreo cookie tweet ("You can still dunk in the dark") during the accidental lighting failure of the 2013 Super Bowl defined a new form of instantaneous event-driven advertising. Coca-Cola's YouTube video of drones delivering cases of Coca-Cola to immigrant high-rise construction workers in Singapore illustrated another type of innovative video advertising in the digital age.

– *Madison Avenue Manslaughter,*
Michael Farmer

Historians mark the end of World War II as the beginning of the global boom in advertising.

INTELLIGENT PRE-SAVING

One of the most important things to understand about human beings is their tendency to spend all the money in their pockets, whether a little or a lot. The consumer society invites us to do so constantly. Most of the things we purchase are not even things that we need. Going against the established system requires a strong will; a will that we do not all share. People do try to save, but the little they manage to put aside often ends up vanishing without so much as an explanation. That's why saving does not work. The secret is pre-saving.

Pre-saving is to ask your bank to deduct a part of your wages at the beginning of each month and have it deposited automatically into a savings account without additional worry or bother. This way, the bank saves for you. Since the money never reaches your pockets, it cannot be spent. Pre-saving is the first step in building the financial freedom we so greatly lack. At the beginning, deducting a tenth of your wages would be ideal.

Start pre-saving for your next adventure now and enjoy the financial freedom it brings.

– Ten Peor Coche que Tu Vecino,
Luis Pita

TIME TO TRANSFORM

Four things that collaborative human social behaviour gives rise to:

- The ability to inspire and be inspired
- The instinctive ability to trust and mistrust
- Feelings of shame and pride
- The willingness to make sacrifices for the greater good.

It is these uniquely human characteristics that allow us to work together successfully in organizations: to be inspired by a common purpose, to trust our colleagues and to want to be seen to be doing our bit, to feel pride in being part of something bigger than ourselves and to be prepared to even make personal sacrifices to achieve this. These human qualities are at the heart of any emotionally healthy organization – and only emotionally healthy organizations will survive in the modern age.

Steam-engine organizations assume – implicitly or explicitly – that these emotions have no place in the workplace – that they are confusing distractions from the rational business of running an efficient enterprise. How wrong they are. These 'emotional' reactions are the very stuff that binds people together in common endeavours.

– *My Steam Engine Is Broken,*
Dr Mark Powell & Jonathan Gifford

The modern organization has become completely outmoded, but we have failed to notice this.

DRIVING KNOWLEDGE

In knowledge-driven firms, people make decisions. Most decisions require a choice on conflicting goals. By definition, contradictory goals need a decision. Conflicts cannot be solved in any other way. As such, decisions require an instance that decides. And who decides becomes liable. Conflicting goals are the right of executives. As Peter F. Drucke said, with the knowledge age, employees become executives. They make decisions.

The challenge for corporate leadership is to guide the decision-making in an organization. What helps your leaders and managers to decide on competing goals? In general, the vision provides a long-term perspective to gauge the decision content (what). Values help on the decision-making process (how). As guidelines, vision and values should create unambiguity! But, values by nature are ambiguous. When we claim 'transparency', we also include 'secrecy'. We make the case for transparency as a value, because some things need to be secret otherwise there would be no reason for having such a value. But complexity cannot be reduced to A or B. Explicit values need to reduce bipolarity. This explains that defining values and vision is difficult and requires utmost care.

As a rule of thumb, some 'non-transparency' helps with values.

– The Performance Triangle,
Lukas Michel

BLOCKCHAIN EXPLAINED

The Double Spend Problem

Imagine two friends in a street, Peter and Paul. Peter has an apple and Paul does not. Peter gives his apple to Paul. The two friends do not need a third party to validate this transaction – Paul can see that he now has the apple and Peter no longer does. Because the apple is a tangible item, those in the transaction are able to self-validate its movement.

Since digital currency is not tangible like an apple – or a coin – it is possible to spend the same digital token twice, unless validation systems are put in place. Traditionally these systems have been middlemen – for example banks. But blockchain technology allows users of the network to validate their own network – as the ledger containing all transactions is shared between them and is visible to everyone. This shared ledger guards against bitcoins (or other digital currencies) appearing from nowhere.

You don't need hierarchies when blockchain allows peers to check the act of others.

– Don Tapscott for *Dialogue*

GLOBAL OPPORTUNITIES

Since the liberalization of its economy in the 1980s, China has become increasingly integrated into the global economy and has moved from the periphery to the centre of the international system. Chinese enterprises are in the news – devouring natural resources, soaking up investment, expanding their overseas footprint and broadening the country's global media exposure and cultural presence. Having experienced net capital inflows for more than 30 years, by 2006 China had accumulated the world's largest foreign exchange reserves, overtaking Japan; it became the world's second largest economy by 2010 (after the United States), and its economy is expected to surpass that of the US by 2025.

China's global expansion did not occur by happenstance. It grew out of government policies launched at the famous Third Plenary Session of the 11th Central Committee in December 1978 to engage in 'reform and opening'. Throughout the 1980s, China 'invited the world in' and took its first small steps on the world stage.

Unclear strategy leads to uninformed moves towards internationalization.

– *Global Expansion,*
Weiru Chen, Yuan Ding,
Klaus Meyer, Gao Wang
& Katherine Xin

MAXIMUM CREATIVITY

It is now more necessary than ever to discover new possibilities, connections and subtle and unexplored relationships (previously superficial and obvious). This will allow us to go beyond problems and contexts, until new ideas translate into solutions, products, services and projects or new lines of business.

Designpedia is a creativity and innovation manual, a collection of tools geared towards the resolution of problems based on the principles of design. If we accept creativity as an innate power that can be developed within people (akin to memory or muscles), it can be defined as the ability to generate new associations between familiar ideas and concepts, in order to produce original solutions ('original' meaning 'unique').

Companies need the capacity to conceptualize design. With simple tools, they are able to bring about innovation in a fast and systematic fashion, implying that they can identify the value for clients and/or users with controlled resources. The ultimate goal is the solid description of concepts and ideas that can be developed and implemented. Though built on uncertainty, their results can be proven with concrete and simple facts.

– *Designpedia,*
Juan Gasca & Rafael Zaragozá

What thought process and type of conceptualization does your company carry out to facilitate and accelerate its development?

DRAWING COMMUNICATION

From the smallest firms to the multinationals, many companies today incorporate dynamic visualization in their day-to-day activities to maximize the concept of work in progress.

The methodologies of visual thinking favour working quickly, cheaply and without risks. Nowadays, it is essential to readily access an overview of all the elements that must be taken into account in order to make the most relevant decisions.

The mapping of a project, the description of usage scenarios, the design of processes, the description of the customer journey, or the prototyping of low and high loyalty, are some of the applications of design-thinking methodologies. In all of these steps, drawing up concepts acts as a core resource.

Furthermore, when taking into account the speed at which the market evolves, it is necessary to work without having to spend a large budget to produce beta models. Thanks to these methodologies, designs take shape in a more direct way, until conceptualization is completed and agreed upon.

Try visual thinking in order to explore all the possibilities of a project and make more informed decisions.

The ideas drawn in a notebook add up and can be used as a good repository of quick reference resources.

– *¡Dibújalo!,*
Fernando de Pablo & Miren Lasa

FOX OR HEDGEHOG?

British philosopher Isaiah Berlin distinguishes between people who strive for a coherent world-view with logic and an organising principle (hedgehogs), and others who are comfortable with loose ends and with not relating things systematically to a bigger picture (foxes).

In essence, this animal metaphor describes fundamental differences in human beings, concerning their preferences regarding organising and processing information and experience. Above all, it teaches us not to blame others for not seeing the world 'correctly', instead, urging us to respect different styles of relating to the world around us.

Management writers Jim Collins and John Kay argue for a hedgehog concept as a key success factor for companies, describing how effective decision makers recognise the limits of their knowledge. Statistical data guru Nate Silver, conversely, has argued that hedgehogs are too often caught up in their models.

There are many more hedgehogs than foxes in top management positions, today. But, since foxes are more able to sense ambiguity and paradox, is this the optimal choice given our turbulent times?

– Timo Meynhardt,
Carolin Hermann &
Stefan Anderer for *Dialogue*

"The fox knows many things, but the hedgehog knows one big thing."
– Antiochus

CHALLENGING TIMES

There is little doubt that retailing around the world is experiencing some of the most interesting and challenging times in its history. There are the global economic changes with low or no growth economies in the West, fast-growing markets in the East and new growth across Africa. Additionally, consumer markets are at the mercy of political shifts, whether through the rise of the middle classes or the search for greater democracy.

No shift is, however, more profound than the rise of the internet economy and the next wave of change largely attributable to the rise of digitally enabled consumers. One might have expected that the internet would by now have simply become business as usual for retailers whose adaptability to the changing consumer is second to none. However, the behavioural shift associated with the digital era is arguably so profound that it requires retailers not simply to act differently, but to think differently, and even to challenge the organisational and cultural structures on which they have been traditionally built.

Retailers are faced with the challenge of keeping up with new innovations disrupting the market.

– Rethinking Retail in The Digital Era,
Brian Kalms & Elix-IRR

LEADERSHIP OR AUTHORITY?

We had to face the mountain, the snow, hunger and cold. Several people stepped into the void and took charge of what was happening. Without knowing the solution, they committed themselves to the group and bound their actions to the group's results. The act of leadership is a disruptive activity. It leads to conflict, to break with inertia, to face different challenges, to face situations that the group doesn't know how to handle. In our case, there was no order telling us to start consuming the bodies of our friends. The group had to solve the situation in a collective discussion, until the group came to an agreement. In any case, what mattered was the example already set by the first group of people, but no one was obliged to follow.

The first signs of leadership in action are recognizing that we do not know we need help, that we cannot move forward alone, and that we need contributions and input from others. This implies sending back the problem to those who initiated it so that the group can work and move forward – with trial and error, and success and learning. We must recognize that when we face an adaptive challenge, authority does not work.

– Into the Mountains: the Extraordinary True Story of Survival in the Andes and its Aftermath, Pedro Algorta

If you let it, trial and error will lead to success and learning for true personal growth.

CASUALTY

We are becoming unthinkingly reliant – addicted – to ease-of-use at the expense of quality. We are walking dumpsters for internet content that we don't need and which might actively damage our brains.

As long ago as 2005, Cornell University researcher Brian Wansink found that people who ate soup from bowls that constantly refilled themselves consumed 73% more than those who ate out of normal bowls. Yet they felt no more satisfied. This 'bottomless bowl' phenomenon is the effect Netflix has when it auto-plays the next episode of a show after a cliffhanger and you continue watching, thinking, "I can make up the sleep over the weekend." The cliffhanger is, of course, always replaced by another cliffhanger. We spend longer in front of the television, yet we feel no more satiated. Perhaps we should go back to our smartphones and, instead of playing Netflix or searching Facebook, use their core function. Call up our friends and have a chat or – better – arrange to meet them.

The TV seems like a puny adversary compared to the deadening digital army we face today.

Too much tech is ruining lives.

– Vivek Wadhwa for *Dialogue*

VOTE AND MANIPULATION

We all know that democracy is a model of social organization within which people freely choose their governing bodies. Individuals, apparently, are free to support those they like, and with our vote we decide our leaders' lines of action, the future of our country and our role in the world. Human beings, however, are not as free nor as prepared to choose their rulers as we believe. It has been shown that the majority of our decisions to support or reject candidates are predominantly emotional and unconscious. This predisposes us to be influenced, pressed and manipulated to support political parties that have little to offer us. The candidates who offer the most to people do not win political campaigns. Those who manipulate people do.

In recent years, neuroscientific studies have shown us that the brains of those who support right and left parties have distinct regions at work. Now we know that when we talk about politics with friends who seem unable to understand our ideas, it may be because their brain has a different way of processing information.

By recognizing what is likely to influence us and being open to the viewpoints of others, we can make more informed choices.

– *Quiero tu Voto* ,
Pedro Bermejo

CHIEF WELLBEING OFFICER

The efficacy of executive function tasks has a close link to health. Research has shown that sleep deprivation does not significantly affect routine thinking, but it does have a great impact on non-routine executive thinking. Exercise has been shown to specifically benefit the frontal lobe part of the brain charged with executive function tasks. Such benefits dissipate after a few days, however, showing the need that busy business leaders have in continually investing in exercise.

So how should we act on such knowledge in business? Of course, we can try and change our own behaviour, yet the greatest impact may come from trying to implement such an approach in the leadership of our teams. Being an executive will almost always mean influencing and directing others – in many instances a great number of others. If in such leadership activity we include notions of health and wellbeing, we can transform the performance of those teams.

In an increasingly technological, digital, always-on world, it seems that the human factor will, after all, still be critical. And health and wellbeing will likely be an ever-greater driver of executive function.

Promoting health and wellbeing in the workplace can transform both individual and team performance.

– *Chief Wellbeing Officer,*
Steven P. Macgregor
& Rory Simpson

THE ENTREPRENEURIAL STATE

Nation-states must become 'entrepreneurial states' – a place where innovations can grow into viable businesses and be backed. This means the focus of public spending must be channelled away from traditional welfare and towards wealth creation.

Professor Mariana Mazzucato points out that states do have some pedigree in fostering entrepreneurialism which has, many years later, paid off, as the discoveries from that research are turned into wealth-creating ventures by enterprising companies. Equally important is the need to switch the emphasis of social security from employment protection to support for self-help and independent, entrepreneurial forms of work. The net aim must be to build a supportive environment for entrepreneurs, along with better-developed capabilities for fostering market-based solutions when and where they make sense, and new public-private or community-based hybrids where they do not.

With digital technology reducing barriers to entry by providing ready-made infrastructures and support services globally on demand, there may not be a better moment in history to democratize entrepreneurship and make it the driving force for democratic capitalism, fostered by an entrepreneurial state.

The net aim must be to build a supportive environment for entrepreneurs.

– Richard Straub for *Dialogue*

CONVERSATION TECHNIQUE

A bore talks only about himself, a gossip only about others. But a skilled conversationalist talks about you – with you. He will get you hooked from the very first. You've certainly tried to talk with somebody who only gives yes or no answers.

Perhaps you have met a monologue monster, one of those people who don't let anyone else get a word in edgeways. If you try to say something, they smile, raise their voice and continue. They cut you off, draw parallels to themselves and fill in sentences you have begun. They have not mastered the art of listening. They break all the conversation taboos there are and the 'conversation' is either very short, or murderously long. If you like talking, there is a risk that you yourself may be a monologue monster. Or perhaps you might have problems taking your share, or finding exciting subjects to talk about.

When it comes to conversation technique, it is actually the introvert who is better off than the extrovert, since introverts tend to master the art of listening. But it's a balancing act. If you are too introverted, sometimes you can be the one who listens without others realizing it. The goal is that people should understand that you are listening and they should want to listen to you.

When a conversation really works, it can be magical.

– *Read My Lips,*
Elaine Eksvärd

NEGOTIATION

Negotiating transforms us. "We play a lot," said an executive who urged us to prepare the negotiation. And, as a matter of fact, we do play a lot. That makes negotiating a task that does not leave us indifferent. Our emotions before the negotiation will be dependent on our previous experience, the knowledge we have of the subject and the other party. But both the type of emotional disruptions and the intensity of them will also depend purely on personal traits. Aspects such as communication style, cultural affiliation, the degree of self-esteem, self-knowledge and, of course, the skills for controlling and expressing emotions will influence the watermark that emotions imprint on the negotiator's interpersonal presence.

The good news is that, although negotiation is an activity that alters us and can hardly be faced with a degree of tranquility or desired control, we can learn to prevent and manage our emotions, so that they do not significantly interfere with the result intended.

If we can learn to manage our emotions effectively it will positively affect our negotiations.

– El Negociador Efectivo,
Mercedes Costa

REAL LUXURY

One of the signs of the prevailing confusion and the chaotic marriage between luxury and consumption can be felt in communications. Historically, the territory and expression of luxury have been the idealized dream, giving clients an emotional and sensory benefit, as opposed to the consumer market which, above all, highlights the tangible benefits of products. The luxury market has been busy fulfilling desires, consumption and needs. Consumption is encouraged with ideal worlds. Needs are disguised with rational arguments.

From the beginning, luxury advertising's central argument has been the product. Only perfect products are displayed, photographed impeccably, as if a work of art. Reasons were not necessary, since in reality telling and explaining what beauty is makes no sense. The mission of the luxury market's communications, excluding technical sectors such as cosmetics or automobiles, has always been focused on teaching the outlook the brand has on the world. It is this quality which induces clients to opt for the imaginary. However, this approach is also changing.

Luxury products communicate the fulfillment of desire.

– *La Fórmula del Lujo,*
Susana Campuzano

LEADING TO A 'T'

Neuroscientist Dr Vivienne Ming asserts that while even complex tasks once performed by experts will be done better by machines, "only one job description for the future matters – creative, adaptive problem-solver".

Applying the human touch, empathy, curiosity and creative problem-solving reminds me of the 'T-Shaped Leader', as first coined by chief executive Tim Brown from IDEO, a firm well known for its human-centred innovation work.

The vertical stroke of the 'T' is a depth of skill in business or technical specialization that allows people to contribute to the creative process because of what they know. The horizontal stroke refers to the breadth of understanding across the business and having a disposition for collaboration across disciplines. T-shaped leaders bring depth of knowledge and breadth of understanding.

In coming years, the depth of the vertical portion of the 'T' might shift from years of accumulated wisdom in a single discipline, to the ability to access, interpret and contextualize insights provided by machines. The top of the 'T' will merit a more prominent position because there will be a premium on leaders who have more of these creative, adaptive, problem-solving skills.

'Creative, adaptive problem-solver', is the job description of the future.

– Michael Canning for *Dialogue*

FAILURE AND INNOVATION

So, what is innovation? It's the act of blazing a trail through unexplored and undeveloped territory. If a company does not tolerate or encourage failure, or reward those who have the courage to take risks but end up stumbling, how can it overtake or overthrow its competitors? How can it enter no man's land strategically? Ren Zhengfei talks about how Huawei must focus all its strength – the so-called 'Van Fleet Load' – on strategic opportunities. He also notes that a considerable part of the 'load' will be spent on 'valuable waste', meaning that exploration in uncharted territory doesn't come without a price.

Heroes emerged in droves during Huawei's first ten years of business, back when it didn't matter who a hero was or where they came from. As long as someone had the courage to try, the company would let them go out and challenge the impossible. Many employees became experts and presidents in their early 20s, developing rapidly through trial and error. The practice of continuously learning and self-correcting, and being undeterred by one mistake after another, has given rise to hordes of outstanding managers and world-class R&D experts who've paved the way for Huawei's success.

Management can never accomplish perfection by standing still.

– Pioneers: Huawei Stories,
Tian Tao & Yin Zhifeng

GAMIFICATION AND SERIOUS GAMES

Games allow us to convert boring actions, or those that leave us indifferent, into something exciting, capable of changing our mindset and behaviour. This led them to cross over to entertainment, while little by little penetrating new worlds, such as education, social inclusion, health, sports, the army or even companies where virtually nobody dares to question if they are here to stay. To achieve this, they have relied on two techniques: gamification and serious games.

Gamification consists of using the mechanics and dynamics of game design in non-leisure spaces. Gamification seeks to make us experience emotions like the ones we experienced when we were children. This playing increases our attachment to the task (training, commitment to the company, motivation for work, etc.). Serious games, also called educational games or those designed with a purpose other than fun, are created to convey information, knowledge or experiences. In short, while gamification transposes the mechanisms of the game to real world problems, serious games transpose the real world onto the terrain of the game.

By transposing the mechanisms of the game to real world problems, gamification can increase our ability to learn.

– *e-Renovarse o Morir,*
Silvia Leal

KNOW HOW TO INVEST

Even when an economic scenario continues to be complicated, it is important to remember that the world will eventually enter a stage of recovery and thereafter of greater growth, making today the best time to invest. Always keep a long-term investment horizon. In fact, for household portfolios, periods of crises open up interesting opportunities to significantly increase the value of investment portfolios. But you have to know how to invest. You have to invest wisely. Experience alone is not enough to guarantee good results. You need a disciplined investment approach. This allows you to control the risk throughout each of its phases rather than in isolation from each other.

The efficient management of an investment portfolio requires an approach that starts with explicitly clarifying the financial objective of the investor, so that once the objective is identified, you can design and customize the structure of the investment portfolio consistent with that objective. The diversification and the analysis of performance are complements of this process, which will lead to satisfactory results in the long term.

In times of economic of uncertainty, it's good to be open and take a long-term investment view that takes advantage of the new opportunities.

– *Mexico Frente a la Crisis,*
Manuel Guzmán

THE INTEGRAL MEDIUM

Digital advertising offers better value, is more efficient and is better targeted than other channels.

By June 2016, China reached 710 million active internet users, approximately half its population and, of the vast and growing time Chinese consumers allocate to internet use, 1hr 27mins a day is spent on social media.

Aligning consumers with social media is a powerful way of promoting products, vendors and merchants doing business on JD.com.

It also allows us to reach customers – and not only core customers who had bought products over the last year, but also to two further groups: so-called 'engagement users', who had commented on, followed or liked the official WeChat page; and 'fans' of the brand – those who had followed or liked news from the brand ambassador.

Direct promotion to target groups over 24 hours resulted in 20,000 new followers – as many as would normally be expected in two months – while sales were five to six times the norm.

Retailers and social networks that have led the way in targeted social campaigns stand to be at the forefront as that exciting change plays out. Stay tuned.

Intelligent, integrated social media campaigning is a powerful marketing force.

– Joey Bian for *Dialogue*

WILLINGNESS TO COMMUNICATE

Meetings have helped guide us through generations – through revolutions and wars, with world leaders and communities. In many eras of our existence, people meeting with each other provided the glue that kept communities strong and focused; sometimes from sheer necessity of saving lives and sometimes for the sheer joy of being with like-minded people.

With our vibrant history in mind, it is disappointing to see that in business, meetings have become lacklustre and in many places 'the grey meeting routine' prevails. In these places meetings are habitual and routine, and serve very little purpose. Unlike great wisdoms that are handed down through generations with care, meetings have been passed down through the years like a game of 'Chinese whispers' where all sense and reason have become lost.

Despite this, meetings are very much alive today. They are alive with human beings. Teams; groups; co-workers; managers; sports teams; boy scouts; parish councils; local councils. Meetings take place in scout huts; church halls; hotels; purpose-built meeting spaces; they happen face-to-face; by phone; online; via webcam.

Decide to adapt your meetings. Decide to communicate well in them. Decide to make them intentional and purposeful.

– *The Meeting Book,*
Helen Chapman

BUSINESS MIRAGE

When we are asked what the most important goal or purpose of a company is, the immediate response would have to be to EARN MONEY. Without a doubt, this is the most important objective. This is why the company exists and the purpose for which it was created.

The problem begins when the company runs solely and exclusively with a cash flow and does not consider the income statement. What results from this is that the director of the company relies on a mirage. Since money is always circulating for payments or advance payments from clients, and the feeling exists that this money is available to be continually spent, no one ever knows the actual level of cash flow in the company's account. The same applies to money allocated to expenses or investments which derives from the suppliers of products or services working with the company.

The idea is to build a true mirror that helps to reflect the financial reality of the company – something that does not confuse by generating the sensation of abundance and, thereby, in reality generating waste.

Understanding the true financial health of a company allows for more efficient use of money and resources.

– *Pequeñas Empresas Grandes Instituciones,* Patricia González

QUESTION TIME

Peter Drucker argued that it was good to play ignorant. Clever people, he implied, make all sorts of assumptions and therefore miss the big questions.

"The most serious mistakes are not being made as a result of wrong answers," he once observed. "The truly dangerous thing is asking the wrong questions."

Never have his teachings mattered more.

The Institute of Leadership & Management is helping managers be ready for a volatile, disrupted world where leaders expect more seminal changes in the next three years than have occurred in the last 30.

One key challenge is that day-to-day grind can push the important strategic questions off the agenda.

"Why are we doing this?"

"Should we be doing this?"

"What networks do we need to form to help us to achieve our goal?"

"How could we do this differently and better?"

Experts are united by one thing: remedies are found by asking the right questions.

The remedy to this most challenging of ages is found by asking the right questions.

The world has changed. But Drucker's teaching is timeless.

– Phil James for *The Drucker Forum Special Report 2017*

AMUSING INTERPRETATION

Insights: 1. Things we have learned, or now understand. 2. Massive unexpected developments; things we had no knowledge of before at all; Road to Damascus-style revelations; blinding flashes of the patently obvious; patronizing summing up of extended away day diatribe, as in: *"I'd like to thank Keith for his valuable insights there."*

Insightful: 1. Full of insight. 2. Horrible bastard son of insight; another in a long line of words with –ful placed at the end to generate a lazy adjective that invariably adds nothing to understanding, as in: *"Thanks for your highly insightful comment, Bernard."*

– *The Business Bullshit Dictionary,*
Kevin Duncan

What the hell are these people talking about?

THE DILEMMA

The first thing that needs to be clarified is that it's not necessary for the child to be the one to succeed the father in a family business. The companies succeeding in separating management from ownership – thus, choosing the most suitable administrator from among professionals – while allowing family members to retain ownership, prove to be the most successful over time. Some families actually go to great lengths to prohibit family members from holding positions in the company, whether or not they are suitable for given roles.

While it is more common for a father to decide that his son, usually the firstborn, should run the business, some place the child in direct competition with the rest of the managers to prove his competence. His son's status will neither place him in an advantageous position nor in an especially inconvenient one either.

Each strategy has pros and cons. A successful decision will turn into profits for the family and the company, and vice versa. But it must be clear that preparing the successor is the duty of every executive.

It may be necessary to put feelings aside to decide the ideal successor in a family business.

– Ser y Hacer de las Familias Empesarias. Una visión integral,
Carlos Llano Cifuentes

TRUE GRIT

How do we improve our capacity to learn? Learning has two dimensions: personal energy and passion, and an ability to demonstrate a growth mindset. Psychologists call this virtuous combination 'grit'. Grit is a better predictor of long-term personal, educational and leadership success than IQ, EQ or sociability.

Attaining grit means setting realistic expectations, taking risks and seeing change as opportunity not threat. When trying something new, it often won't work and it is very easy to blame and rationalize. Grit, however, means facing mistakes, running into them and honestly evaluating what worked and what did not work, then learning from that criticism. Likewise, successes must be relished, credit shared and emphasis always kept on 'why' it worked.

Grit is not content to remain stagnant: build on your strengths, find lessons and inspiration in the success of others and surround yourself with friends who are learning and growing.

The simplest way to achieve grit, however, is to start small: think big, test small, fail fast and learn, always.

Successful leaders are passionate and focus resolutely on growth.

– Dave Ulrich for *Dialogue*

VOCABULARY REVISIONS

Vocabitude is the lexicon of words we use with each attitude. If you are despondent and gloomy, your brain will push certain vocabulary to the front and you will find yourself using words such as loss, defeat, pointless, whatever, don't know, don't care, why, why not and no!

If you are full of energy, confidence and belief, your words are more likely to include can, will, let's, how, what, possible, chance and yes!

a) Over the week ahead, tune in to the words of others when you know the mood and attitude they are in, then tune into your own.

b) Develop your Vocabitude – the words you use when you are at the top of your attitude range.

c) Have them to hand when you are feeling off beat and insert them in your written and spoken conversations (especially if, at first, they feel incongruous to your bad mood).

Give your attitude a great script.

– *The Attitude Book,*
Simon Tyler

DESTRUCTIONISM

The systematic practice of coercion on business activities, the most intimate essence of socialism – or, perhaps even better, of 'statism', whether from the left or right – blocks human creativity and its ability to coordinate. It wreaks havoc on the process of social cooperation, destroys multiple sources of wealth and generates all kinds of conflicts, violence, poverty and misery everywhere.

That is why Mises, in his book *Critique of Interventionism*, which analyses the role of the state in the economy, calls the socialist system 'destructionism', in view of the perverse effects it generates. Fortunately, and in spite of the havoc it continually causes, socialism has never managed to completely eliminate the impulse that the free business initiatives humans generate have made possible the development of civilizations. If Evil (as defined by the destructionism of Mises's terminology) had triumphed, mankind and civilization would have disappeared long ago. (In fact, we could claim that it is precisely what the Malefic desires when he encourages – using every type of deception and decoys – destructionist policies: to end God's work.)

– *Ideas en Libertad,*
Jesús Huerta de Soto

> **Socialism has never managed to completely eliminate the impulse that the free business initiatives humans generate have made possible the development of civilizations.**

AN ESSENTIAL CHALLENGE

A vision is an aspiration, a dream or a mental image, which unites, excites and inspires a group of people seeking a challenge to grow and leave something in their wake.

The vision must be sufficiently challenging and, at the same time, realistic. It is this quest that gives meaning to life and to companies. It is very important because it gives meaning to what we are doing. It makes us get up in the morning with more energy. It gives us clarity and focus on what we want. It guides us in the moments of making decisions. It gives us a sense of achievement. If this vision is so powerful, then why don't all companies have it? Why don't all human beings have it?

The answers are manifold. In the case of companies, having a vision requires focusing on the business and limits management to investing in only that which is necessary. By establishing the vision, you will realize that some businesses don't fit and should be sold off. Another of these answers involves the creation of a culture that matches the business strategy.

It is essential to establish a vision to give meaning and purpose.

– *Your Life, Your Best Business,*
Salvador Alva

FIND ANSWERS

Coaching is a process of a certain duration. It relies on an explicit demand from the client. For the process to be successful, four preconditions must be met:

1. The client must have a desire to grow and be willing to answer questions.
2. The client must be convinced of the effectiveness of coaching and believe in the benefits of the support.
3. The client must have one or several precise and explicit needs: a question that requires immediate and prompt resolution; demand from a company; expertise to acquire; support during a transition period; an improvement of results; or a change needed in relation to other objectives.
4. Good chemistry must flow between client and coach so that they work well with each other. The client must trust the coach.

A coaching contract can last between a few minutes to a few months, even a year or two, depending on whether the topic at hand is timely or not. The length of time depends on the nature of the problem and objectives to be achieved.

– Coaching Excellence:
Best Practices in Business Coaching,
Viviane Launer & Sylviane Cannio

In order to grow we must be willing to take a look in the mirror and answer the difficult questions.

AGES OF LEADERSHIP

Combining my own terminology with that used by Kegan (2009) and Torbert (2004), we arrive at four stages of maturity in a leader of a team as they move from team manager, to team leader, to team orchestrator to team coach.

The first age of a successful professional career is Outer Directed; characterized by trying to meet the goals, targets and expectations of others, chiefly of those senior to yourself. Motivation is pinned on the need to prove yourself and needing those more senior to rate you as successful.

In the second age, Self Authoring, you formulate your own success criteria and become self-directed and directing of others.

The Systemic Orchestrator of the third age listens skilfully to many perspectives. They move from being the hub to the orchestrator, creating synergies across different viewpoints and needs.

On reaching the fourth and final age, Eldership, leaders let go of responsibility and control. Instead they are focused on enabling the leadership of others.

Put yourself in the flow of traffic and pierce your cocoon.

– Peter Hawkins for *Dialogue*

THE PERFECT DICTATORSHIP

The famous episode that put Mario Vargas Llosa at the centre of the Mexican debate occurred in August 1990, in front of millions of television viewers within the framework of a round of First Meetings devoted to the experience of freedom. Octavio Paz and I had brought together about 40 thinkers and authors from around the world (including several Nobel prize winners) to discuss the state of various major issues on the threshold of the 21st century: freedom, religion, nationalism, the economy, justice and socialism.

While Octavio was speaking, Vargas Llosa slipped me a little note asking if I could intervene right away, with a harsher criticism. I agreed, of course, and, after recommending the peaceful suicide of the PRI, I asked Vargas Liosa for his opinion. It was then that, not without apologizing for the possible inelegance of what he was about to say, he coined the famous phrase: "'Mexico is the perfect dictatorship'. The perfect dictatorship isn't Fidel Castro's Cuba: it's Mexico – because it's a dictatorship that's so well camouflaged, it manages not to look like one."

Do you agree with Vargas Llosas that there are no major differences between the traditional dictatorships of Latin American and the Mexican regime?

– *Ideas en Libertad,*
Enrique Krauze

AN ETHICAL MATTER

Entrepreneurs cannot live a double life, one inside their business community and another outside of it. The congruence of their business activities, in accordance with their principles and values, is the best example to inspire and attract others, and honestly advise many. Otherwise the entrepreneur would be wasting his time miserably, perhaps, deceiving others.

Of equal importance is the rectitude of his intentions. Meaning that in each and every one of his daily tasks, in his companies or his relationship with other entrepreneurs, he is always looking for the good in others. The entrepreneur realizes his aspirations when he pursues his vocation in a genuine fashion and is more motivated by it than by personal and material success. When your company and the companies in which you are involved directly or indirectly operate correctly and focus on serving the common good, you make a rich contribution to economic and moral development, and even to the spiritual well-being of all society. Otherwise, it would be useless and even perhaps detrimental to its multiplier effect.

Entrepreneurs should strive to be authentic and genuine to establish a successful brand that serves the common good.

– *Iniciativa Empresarial*
Pilar M. Aguilar &
José Antonio Dávila

MAKE WORK FUN

You can always spice up a tough or mundane day by setting yourself little challenges. For example, getting a certain amount of work done in a particular amount of time, or perhaps before another person. One summer between academic years at university, a group of friends and I worked in a factory. Our job was to unpack boxes of product, stack them up on pallets and then shrink-wrap the pallets to be picked up by the forklift truck driver, who, I was pleased to see, was a woman.

This could have made for very boring long days. Being relentlessly competitive though, my friends and I suggested to the supervisor that if we split into two teams and worked on two pallets at once we could get more pallets packed in less time. We then, of course, raced each other. This made it an awful lot more fun, so we enjoyed it and the supervisor was happy because we got a lot more pallets stacked. I think that's called a win–win situation.

– Work-Life Symbiosis,
Claire Fox

There are always positives, as long as you look for them.

MAKING A CONNECTION

When we make eye contact with another human, there is no doubt that we are making a connection with each other. The cliché of eyes meeting across a crowded room is such a powerful one because of this primal, interpersonal connection. Two people know, in that moment, that they are occupying a shared space in each other's minds.

Eyes also express intention. Think of aiming a bow and arrow at a mark on a tree. Imagine looking at the point on the tree that you hope to hit with your arrow and pulling your arm back. Just before you let the arrow loose, can you feel what happens with your focus?

There's an increase in attention and all other noises and sights fade out, increasing your chances of hitting your target. Using your eyes to deliver an idea, with the same intent you would use to shoot an arrow, adds power to your speech in the same way. If you don't look at the people you are speaking to, you have no idea if your words have hit their mark.

This does not mean you need to look at your audience or single listener continuously as you speak. You only need to look at them as you say the last few words of an important thought.

Don't take your shot and then look away!

– *The Connection Book,*
Emma Serlin

FINANCIAL EDUCATION

The knowledge necessary to make good financial decisions doesn't demand an extraordinary effort from individuals. Anyone can learn basic concepts and operations to manage their money in a prudent and responsible manner. One of the biggest challenges of financial education is to break down the prejudice that the topic is only for experts, for financiers or people with high economic assets. It is overlooked that basic knowledge of well-applied personal finance contributes significantly to improving quality of life, regardless of the socioeconomic status of the people. Therefore, it is essential to raise awareness about the value of financial education from an early age for all economic classes.

Those with better and more information will have an advantage. They can compare different products and services on offer by different banking intermediaries. If users of financial services are better informed, they will be able to demand better quality products and services and stimulate innovation and competition among financial institutions. Competition, in turn, stimulates the development of the market and financial services and ultimately leads to a positive impact on the national economy.

– *Educación Financiera para México*, Ingrid García de Güémez & Marcella Lembert

Take the time to learn the basic concepts so you can manage your personal finances properly and so protect your assets.

WE NEED TO BE HAPPY

I have never met anyone who did not want to be happy. Many do not recognize it. Others disguise the quest for happiness with generous actions towards others. Even the most lucid find in solidarity the deep satisfaction that makes them happy. No one, however, ever claimed unhappiness. The psychiatrist Luis Rojas Marcos argues that the instinct of happiness is genetic, that we are all born with the ability to protect and seek satisfaction in life. He cites children as an example: "If we leave them alone, they will naturally be happy, because it is in their genes." We seek happiness because we need it, because we respond to the instinct guiding us to it. But often, we also look for it in places where it is not to be found. We get sidetracked.

Commercialism is the usher that leads to frustration. A lack of education in failure, which is part of the path, is not a defeat; in the same way that adversity is not a parenthesis, but a part of life. A life that has to be lived. Because if we confuse living with lasting, we will be unhappy and we will make others unhappy.

Happiness is woven into healthy relationships: emulation instead of envy, motivation instead of demoralization. Travel with others who are aware of the universal language of love.

Happiness isn't found in things and status but in ourselves and those around us.

– *Hablemos sobre Felicidad* ,
Juan Ramón Lucas, Sandra Ibarra
& Javier Fernández Aguado

THE RIGHT PRESCRIPTION

If we do not get serious about nuclear energy and gas, we can be sure of one thing – there will be more carbon dioxide blanketing the planet in the years to come. Already we have the bizarre situation in which the US, non-believers, are reducing carbon emissions while the zealous Europeans are boosting them. Why? Because the pragmatic Americans are using cheaper domestic gas whereas Europe, with expensive gas but not enough cheap nuclear energy to fall back on, is falling back on cheap coal. And on the course it is setting itself, it can expect more of the same, with Germany already in line for an increase in coal-fired generation because of its irrational aversion to nuclear energy.

Energy planning, by its very nature, is a long-term affair. Unfortunately, it is at the mercy of politicians, for whom no light illuminates any landscape beyond the next election. They will pander to the popular taste for superficially green policies, if they think that is what will win votes, because in the long-term they will be gone. Sadly, the legacies of ill-conceived policies are more enduring than their political architects. Concern about climate change is perfectly rational and legitimate.

Let us do everything we can to keep our planet clean and habitable.

– *The Green Bubble*,
Per Wimmer

CORPORATE SOCIAL RESPONSIBILITY

The entrepreneur, therefore, owner and manager, would have these three purposes:

- Keep the company afloat (with the pursuit of profit)
- Establish itself in the field of social class
- Assume a position of prestige in the community where it operates.

These objectives can be seen as goals that are realized in the course of the life of a business.

A businessperson's first goal is to become profitable and to generate revenues to pay back the resources invested in the company. As this profit becomes stable, assuring continuity and harmony in management, he will want to expand presence in the territory and, therefore, perhaps open new stores, using the experience gained with the first one, and try to become the primary chain of stores in the area the business is operating in.

As time passes by, having steadily achieved profit targets and market power, he will tend to add additional needs, such as to be recognized as the entrepreneur who created jobs, who brought prosperity and the like, so he will search for social prestige, namely recognition by the community where he operates.

Growing means to collaborate and work together.

– Natuzzi,
Luca Condosta

HISTORY DOES NOT CONDEMN

We condition ourselves in the environment where we are based. We can be born and grow up in a healthy and hostile environment, both loving and indifferent, with absent or overprotective parents, with conservative or liberal parents and parents who base their education on fear or respect. Parents involved in a family business want the same future for their children. There are parents who put themselves above their children to meet their own needs.

Although living in these environments, for many, could be a sentence, the truth is that though these factors do influence us, they don't condemn us to reliving the same story, especially when it is not even our own version but one that others have previously assigned. Things are not as bad as they seem. It is not because those who give us life condition us in a certain way that they determine our future.

Our history is unique. But what we have lived so far does not have to become the only life we have. It is always possible to write a new one and reconstruct a better living experience.

It may be necessary to rewrite the way you experience life to achieve personal fulfillment.

– *La Zanahoria es lo de Menos,*
David Montalvo

GLOBALOPHOBE OR GLOBALOPHILE

Globalization is a phenomenon that has divided public opinion like few others. On the one hand, there are the globalophobes who are against it and, on the other, the globalophiles who embrace it. Who is right? To find a good answer, I asked the following question: what is globalization?

Globalization is the process by which governments reduce or eliminate the barriers that, in an arbitrary way, are imposed on people of different nationalities. If successful, the process results in globalization, a world in which governments do not impose artificial barriers on relationships between people. These limit (in the best of cases) or eliminate (in the worst of them) the freedom of people to relate in all possible areas in the manner that suits them best.

Globalization, practised as the reduction or elimination of the barriers which governments impose on relationships between people of different nationalities, is a process of liberation, favouring freedom which, as such, must be supported. The globalophobes, in opposing globalization, are against freedom. The globalophiles, by supporting it, are in its favour.

To oppose globalization is to oppose freedom.

– *Veinte Falacias Económicas,*
Arturo Damm

IT'S ABOUT PLANNING

Despite the plethora of tools and techniques now available to teams, planning is consistently identified by team members as an 'issue' impacting on performance. Teams, reflecting the work styles and personalities of individual members, can often be addicted to action. The need to get things done and quickly move towards the goal can undermine the need to systematically plan. The result of this action orientation can have an impact not just on efficient task accomplishment but also on the relationships within the team.

However, it does need to be acknowledged that, in some organizations, very sophisticated planning practices and policies exist to which teams are obliged to adhere. While in general terms these practices ensure planning is consistently undertaken, teams may find that the methodology is not necessarily the most appropriate for the project or work at hand. Teams can over-plan. They can end up investing time, effort and energy in developing plans, reports and critical path analysis that the work simply does not warrant.

Teams need to be conscious of the potentially negative impacts of both under-planning and over-planning.

Leaders need to encourage early conversations to discuss what planning is needed to deliver the goals.

– Wake Up and Smell the Coffee,
Simon Mac Rory

THE POWER OF MONEY

The way we relate to money determines our values and the part it plays in our lives. The importance money has for us expresses our way of seeing the world. Psychologists point out that dreaming of excrement means money. Maybe because they identify it with something dirty. Constipated people tend to be stingy because they find it very difficult to part with things. Money means power. The powerful need money to feel superior. However, a criminal only needs a weapon. Curiously when criminals steal a lot of money, they waste it. Surveys indicate that for most people who seek work, the type of task to be developed, rather than money, is the first priority.

If money were happiness, the rich would be happy. Nevertheless, often money becomes your worst enemy, dividing families, creating resentment and envy, and more often than not making one the target of kidnappers and thieves. Money can make you a slave to your fortune, which often leads to moral decay.

Not having money is bad, having money is better but having a lot of money is worst.

– *Además, soy Empresario en la Bolsa,*
Carlos Ponce B.

MOTIVATED PEOPLE

Execution basically comes down to the quality and motivation of the people involved in the start-up. I strongly recommend starting up at a good moment in your life. This will need to be a time when you can spend a lot of your energy on the project. It might make sense to avoid, for example, when you have a new-born baby or when you are going through a divorce, or for that matter, getting married. I also highly recommend getting high-quality people on board early on. For one thing, it's much more fun being in a group of people, sharing both the downs of the failures and the ups of the successes. Being an entrepreneur is a deeply bipolar process. You will have more mood swings than a Hollywood actress. Secondly, good people will also increase vastly your chance of success. It is important not to be miserly with shares in your company. Give them a piece of the action. Very few things are as motivational as having your own skin in the game.

Factors for success are: how well you execute and making sure you have a major trend behind you.

– *The Environmental Capitalist,* Carl Hall

BRAIN FITNESS

To cultivate a healthy relationship with sleep, it helps to understand your sleep. You probably already know that you sleep in cycles. During every 90-minute cycle, your brain shifts through different stages that correlate with different brain 'states' as measured by EEG (electroencephalography) machines. Broadly speaking, you divide your sleep between periods of deep (slow-wave) sleep and REM (rapid eye movement) sleep.

The first few cycles of sleep, soon after you've fallen asleep, are characterized by a lot of deep sleep, when your body produces the growth hormone. This helps promote physical restoration.

Subsequent sleep cycles, in the latter half of your night's slumber, tend to involve a greater proportion of REM sleep, (associated with dreaming) and this promotes learning, memory and mental restoration.

Five sleep cycles (seven-and-a-half hours) allows for more cognitive restoration than four cycles (six hours), and consequently promotes superior mental function. Less than six hours and you really start to suffer.

With less sleep you may have more time to work, but you have no cognitive competence with which to do it.

– *The Brain Book,*
Phil Dobson

STEREOTYPES

In each historical period, stereotypes have defined the labour division by gender. Since, by biological conditions, a woman possesses the capacity to procreate, it is inferred that she will automatically develop a maternal instinct. Man is given other models related to masculinity, such as being a provider, head of the family and representing authority.

The roots of these archetypes evolve in such a way that the 'worth' of women and men – or femininity or virility, respectively – is measured through them. With the passage of time, societies cultivate these templates and thus determine what should be the ideal behaviour of men and women.

The problem is that these behaviours were not chosen and accepted individually, but are part of cultural heritage or family legacy. They condition the development of human capabilities and inhibit those who 'socially' do not belong to their gender.

This is the origin of the discrimination. The relationship between men and women and how they are treated is conditioned by the behaviours that are expected from one and the other.

– La Nueva era de los Negocios, Mujeres Rumbo a la alta Dirección, María del Carmen Bernal González & Alejandra L. Moreno Maya

The problem of gender roles is that they were not chosen or accepted individually, but are part of cultural heritage that needs to be challenged.

STOP ADDING VALUE

It is extremely difficult for successful people to listen to other people tell them something that they already know without communicating somehow that they a) already knew that and b) know a better way.

Imagine I come to you with an idea that you think is very good. Rather than just pat me on the back and say, "Great idea!" your inclination – because you have to add value – is to say, "Good idea, but it would be better if you tried it this way."

You may have improved the content of my idea by 5%, but you've reduced my commitment to executing it by 50%, because you've taken away my ownership of the idea. My idea is now your idea – and I walk out of your office less enthused about it than when I walked in. That's the fallacy of added value. Whatever we gain in the form of a better idea is lost many times over in our employees' diminished commitment to the concept.

Get out your notepad. Instead of your usual 'To Do' list, start your 'To Stop' list.

Leaders need to know when to shut up.

– Marshall Goldsmith
for *Dialogue*

THE RULES OF
THE GAME

We constantly hear that children should not suffer from the traumas of excess repression. This approach facilitates an anxiety-free development but, in excess, makes young people devoid of motivation, who have difficulty in deciding their own future.

Nowadays, parents feel confused and disoriented when they have to educate and set rules. This results in contradictory behaviour. It scares us to disappoint them. We do not know or want to say NO. We do not want to frustrate them. We worry about coming across as authoritarian. We compensate for the lack of time and dedication with an indulgent and guilty stance. We are afraid of conflict and its negative consequences. It seems that we act selfishly if we impose rules that make our lives easier. Well, we are so wrong! The rules help everyone – parents and children alike. Perfect education does not exist, but we can have guidelines to find clarity in different situations.

Setting clear guidelines and boundaries for your children's behaviour avoids confusion.

– Mujer, ¡apuéstale a la Familia!,
Lucía Legorreta

PURPOSE

Leaders need to gather narratives, artefacts, perspectives and ideas that reveal 'latent purpose'. This is an oblique approach of listening in to what people are thinking and feeling – rather than asking them to define the purpose, which is a mistake that many leaders make. Only then can leaders start building the narrative that will eventually morph into organizational purpose.

It begins by paying attention to what people say when they are asked the question, "Why are we here?"

There are two conversations at this stage, the first one being the 'affect' or 'service' conversation. This conversation inquires into the feeling that the organization evokes in its people.

The second conversation is about 'meaning', which elicits the story of the organization and its relevance.

Only after a thorough examination of affect and meaning can leaders turn to the third conversation, 'power', which is about finding the answer to how the sense of purpose can be applied.

With these strategic steps, everyone can develop a clear line of sight with purpose and understanding what they need to do.

A sense of meaning is key to success in a VUCA world.

– Michael Chavez &
Sudhanshu Palsule
for *Dialogue*

ABILITY TO SURVIVE

With the passage of time, most executives become more aware of the business which their company operates in: the opportunities arising, the competition they face, the needs of their clients, the strategic challenges they must confront, among others. But this is not enough. An organization behind the business makes this possible. It is composed of people. An organization has a complex, specific and ever-changing dynamic, whose functioning can make the business a success or failure. If the people who run a company see themselves as helmsmen of a boat sailing turbulent waters, they must recognize that they have at their disposal not only one oar, but two. The one of the business and the one of the organization. To be effective, an executive must be aware of both oars and know how to use them skillfully.

Just as business rowing advocates the usual maximization of profits – in the case of a for-profit company – the rowing of the organization should have as a criterion its ability to adapt. It is essential that any organizational decision be directed towards the increase of this capacity, which is determined by the five basic dimensions that make up the organization: purpose, strategy, structure, culture and talent.

We must develop sufficient adaptive capacity to cope with business challenges.

– *Capacidad Adaptativa,*
Juan Carlos Eichholz

GOING GLOBAL

First, to expand the size of the Wanda enterprise. International investment is required for expansion in some industries, especially in industries such as entertainment and sports, where the foreign market is more advanced than the Chinese one. This is a key reason why Wanda wishes to expand overseas.

Second, to become a global company. In 2015, a resignation letter caused a nationwide sensation in China. A teacher wrote, "The world is so big. I'd like to check it out." I'd like to borrow this sentence to describe Wanda: "The world is so big. I'd like to go make the best of it."

The core of Wanda's corporate culture has always been eight words. When we first established the company in 1988, I suggested using 'Be an Honest Person: Work Smart' as the core of our corporate culture. At that time China had just opened up and there were many frauds in the business world. We honoured honesty and integrity. We advocated 'Be an Honest Person'. And at the same time, we also believed in 'Working Smart'.

No matter how well a country's economy is developing, it will still have periods of economic adjustment.

– *The Wanda Way,*
Wang Jianlin

FLUID ENDINGS

When technology permits innovation, creativity rises to the occasion. As more people use the cloud for reading books, it's possible that, in future, novels might be revised by their authors – or by their readers – and different endings released.

Readers might become participants in shaping a novel.

Yet fiction has a profile disproportionate to the sector's size: it accounts for just 20% of global book revenues. But most publications are nonfiction titles or textbooks and of the ten most profitable publishing houses in the world, only two can be considered publishers of literature. Given this, it is the world of non-fiction that will be transformed most by the cloud.

Cloud reading brings a lot of other advantages: it's cheaper for readers; more profitable for publishers; reduces book piracy since they are not downloadable; and facilitates contact between author/publisher and reader.

True interactivity, true multilateralism, will transform the world of non-fiction.

Will you one day contribute your knowledge to the world of non-fiction?

– Marcelino Elosua for *Dialogue*

INDEX

Sharing knowledge since 1993

- 1993 Madrid
- 2008 Mexico DF and Monterrey
- 2010 London
- 2011 New York and Buenos Aires
- 2012 Bogotá
- 2014 Shanghai